At the Rou Imagined Corners:
A Multicultural Anthology of Contemporary Poetry

Edited by Ken Watson

I do not want my house to be walled in on all sides and my windows to be stifled. I want all the cultures of all lands to be blown about my house as freely as possible. But I refuse to be blown off my feet by any.

Mahatma Gandhi

First published in Australia by St Clair Press 1999
Reprinted in 2005 by Phoenix Education

PHOENIX EDUCATION PTY LTD
Melbourne   **Sydney**
PO Box 197, Albert Park 3206   PO Box 3141, Putney 2112
Tel: (03) 9699 8377 Fax: (03) 9699 9242   Tel: (02) 9809 3579 Fax: (02) 9808 1430
www.phoenixeduc.com

Collection copyright © Ken Watson 1999

All rights reserved. Except as permitted under the Australian Copyright Act 1968 (for example a fair dealing for the purposes of study, research, criticism or review), no part of this book may be reproduced, stored in a retrieval system, or transmitted in any form or by any means without prior written permission. Copyright owners may take legal action against a person or organisation who infringes their copyright through unauthorised copying. All inquiries should be directed to the publisher at the address above.

ISBN 0 949898 93 7

Design and typesetting: by Propaganda/goose
Printed and bound in Australia by Shannon Books

Introduction

The aim of this multicultural anthology is to set beside contemporary verse in English a generous selection of work in translation from a variety of non-English-speaking writers. Appropriately, the poets whose work is presented here in translation come from cultures which have so richly contributed, through immigration, to Australasia in the period since World War II: Italy, Greece, Poland, Hungary, Romania, Yugoslavia, the Czech Republic. Included also are poets from Asia: from India, China, Vietnam.

As far as poets writing in English are concerned, since writers like Ted Hughes, Seamus Heaney and other giants of post-World War II poetry in English already have a firm place in the school curriculum, it was not considered necessary to have them represented here; rather, it seemed important to draw students' attention to some lesser known but critically acclaimed writers in English. As far as writers from non-English-speaking countries were concerned, most chose themselves, since the finest poets are naturally the first choice for translation.

Where appropriate, two translations of the one poem have been included, as this gives students the opportunity to explore the challenges facing translators, and the subtle differences that result from different word choices.

Part 2 of this collection examines the power of traditional story by showing how contemporary poets return again and again to those myths, legends and folk tales which have played such a powerful part in various cultures.

At senior level, rarely is there an opportunity to explore the craft of light verse. This is a pity, because the skill displayed in such writing is often very great indeed, and it is likely that more readers would be won for poetry if the opportunity to explore the work of some of the leading practitioners were given. Hence the last section of this collection includes some examples of light verse.

Where this collection is being used at school or college level, it is strongly recommended that at least some of the poets be represented in the school library so that students can read more widely. The starred items in the Bibliography are appropriate choices for this purpose.

My thanks to Peter Adams and Matthew Brown for their help and advice.

Ken Watson

Contents

Introduction i

Part 1: Sixteen Poets, Fifteen Countries

BEI DAO (Chinese)	*Declaration* trans. Bonnie McDougall	1
	Declaration trans. Fang Dai, D Ding, E Morin	1
	Requiem	2
	A Picture	2
	Landscape Over Zero	3
	Gains	4
	The Bell	4
SUJATA BHATT	*The One Who Goes Away*	5
(Indian)	*The Langur Coloured Night*	6
	What Happened to the Elephant?	8
	Muliebrity	9
	The Stare	9
	Oranges and Lemons	11
	Wine from Bordeaux	12
	Orpheus Confesses to Eurydice	14
NINA CASSIAN	*Evolution*	17
(Romanian)	*Greed*	18
	Longing	19
	Pain	19
	I Wanted to Stay in September	20
	Escape	20
	The Young Bat	22
	The Couple	22
	Ballad of the Jack of Diamonds	23
	Ars Poetica - A Polemic	24
	Snowbound	24
CHARLES CAUSLEY	*Lord Sycamore*	25
(English)	*Recruiting Drive*	26
	Ballad of the Bread Man	27
	Ballad of the Faithless Wife	29
	The Question	30
	At the British War Cemetery, Bayeux	31
	I Am the Great Sun	32

CAROL ANN DUFFY	*What Price?*	33
(Scottish)	*Head of English*	34
	Never Go Back	35
	Close	36
	Originally	37
	Yes Officer	38
	Selling Manhattan	39
	Nostalgia	40
ODYSSEUS ELYTIS	*Aegean*	41
(Greek)	*from The Gloria*	42
	The Sleep of the Brave	44
	"With what stones, what blood, and what iron…"	45
	"All day long we walked in the fields…"	47
	The Mad Mad Boat	48
U A FANTHORPE	*Casehistory: Alison (head injury)*	49
(English)	*Reports*	50
	BC:AD	51
	You will be hearing from us shortly	51
	Not My Best Side	53
	Sunderland Point and Ribchester	55
	Halley's Comet 1985-86	57
	Nativities	58
MIROSLAV HOLUB	*Brief Reflection on Accuracy*	60
(Czech)	*Brief Thoughts on Exactness*	61
	Brief Reflection on Laughter	62
	Brief Thoughts on Laughter	63
	Brief Thoughts on a Test-Tube	64
	Brief Reflection on Test-Tubes	65
	Minotaur's Thoughts on Poetry	66
	The Minotaur's Thoughts on Poetry	67
	The Soul	68
	Swans in Flight	68
IVAN LALIĆ	*How Orpheus Sang*	69
(Serbo-Croat)	*Ophelia*	70
	Requiem for a Mother	71
	Of Eurydice	72
	Letter from the Knight Sinadin	73
	Princip on the Battlefield	74
	The Argonauts	74
	Young Woman from Pompeii	75
	The Spaces of Hope	76

GWYNETH LEWIS	*Peripheral Vision*	77
(Welsh)	*Flyover Elegies I, II*	78
	Fax X	79
	The Reference Library	79
	Pentecost	80
	Good Dog	81
MUDROOROO	*A Righteous Day*	83
(Australian Aboriginal)	*The Ultimate Demonstration*	84
	Tracks	85
	Who?	85
	Quietness	86
	Hide and Seek	87
	City Suburban Lines	87
DENNIS O'DRISCOLL	*In Office*	89
(Irish)	*Fruit Salad*	90
	Operation	92
	Looking Forward	93
	Case Studies	93
	Elegies	95
	Premonitions	96
	What She Does Not Know Is	96
JÁNOS PILINSZKY	*Fable*	97
(Hungarian)	*Fish in the Net*	98
	The French Prisoner	99
	Passion of Ravensbruck	100
	The Desert of Love	101
	Revelations VIII.7	102
	Gradually	102
TADEUSZ RÓŻEWICZ	*Mars*	103
(Polish)	*The Survivor*	104
	Abattoirs	105
	Posthumous Rehabilitation	105
	A Tree	106
	Massacre of the Boys	107
	Pigtail	107
	Grass	108
	What Luck	109
	Re-education	109
	Completion	110
VITTORIO SERENI	*First Fear*	111
(Italian)	*Second Fear*	111
	A Dream	112

	Six in the Morning	112
	Those Children Playing	113
	Madrigal to Nefertiti	114
	Those Thoughts of Yours of Calamity	114
	From Holland: Amsterdam	115
XUAN QUYNH	Worried Over the Days Past	117
(Vietnamese)	The Co May Flower	118
	Wave	119

Part 2: Variations on Traditional Stories

Donald Justice	Orpheus Opens His Morning Mail -	121
Gwen Strauss	Cinderella	122
Sue Stewart	Cinders	123
Gwen Strauss	The Waiting Wolf	123
Sue Stewart	Inside Wolf	125

Part 3 The Craft Of Light Verse

WENDY COPE	Engineers' Corner	127
	Triolet	128
	Reading Scheme	128
SOPHIE HANNAH	Symptoms	129
	Summary of a Western	130
	A Day Too Late	131
	Credit for the Card	131
TIM HOPKINS	Snowy Woods Revisited	132
	The Bystander	133
	What the Papers Say: Othello	134
	Designer Pets	134
	Cat	134
	The Moments in Between	135

Explanatory Notes	137
Cross-Comparisons	143
Other Suggestions for Discussion	144
Bibliography	149
Acknowledgements	151

Bei Dao

Chinese □ 1949-

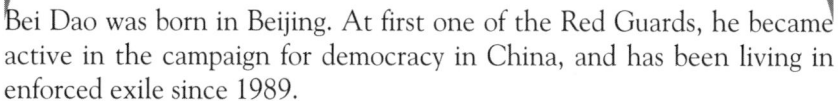

Bei Dao was born in Beijing. At first one of the Red Guards, he became active in the campaign for democracy in China, and has been living in enforced exile since 1989.

Declaration

for Yu Luoke

Perhaps the final hour is come
I have left no testament
Only a pen, for my mother
I am no hero
In an age without heroes
I just want to be a man

The still horizon
Divides the ranks of the living and
    the dead
I can only choose the sky
I will not kneel on the ground
Allowing the executioners to look tall
The better to obstruct the wind of
    freedom

From star-like bullet holes shall flow
A blood-red dawn

(Bonnie McDougall)

Declaration

For the martyr Yu Luoke

Perhaps the last moment is here
I haven't left a will
Only a pen . . . to my mother
I'm not a hero
In an era without heroes
I just wanted to be a man

The quiet horizon
Separated the ranks of the living
    from the dead
I had to choose the sky
And would never kneel on the ground
To let executioners look gigantic
So they could block the wind of
    freedom

Out of starlike bullet holes
A bloody dawn is flowing

(Fang Dai, Dennis·Ding and Edward Morin)

Requiem
for the victims of June Fourth

Not the living but the dead
under the doomsday-purple sky
go in groups
suffering guides forward suffering
at the end of hatred is hatred
the spring has run dry, the conflagration stretches unbroken
the road back is even further away

Not gods but the children
amid the clashing of helmets
say their prayers
mothers breed light
darkness breeds mothers
the stone rolls, the clock runs backwards
the eclipse of the sun has already taken place

Not your bodies but your souls
shall share a common birthday every year
you are all the same age
love has founded for the dead
an everlasting alliance
you embrace each other closely
in the massive register of deaths

(Bonnie McDougall and Chen Maiping)

A Picture
for Tiantian's fifth birthday

Morning arrives in a sleeveless dress
apples tumble all over the earth
my daughter is drawing a picture
how vast is a five-year-old sky
your name has two windows
one opens towards a sun with no clock-hands

the other opens towards your father
who has become a hedgehog in exile
taking with him a few unintelligible characters
and a bright red apple
he has left your painting
how vast is a five-year-old sky

(Bonnie McDougall and Chen Maiping)

Landscape Over Zero

it's hawk teaching song to swim
it's song tracing back to the first wind

we trade scraps of joy
enter family from different directions

it's a father confirming darkness
it's darkness leading to that lightning of the classics

a door of weeping slams shut
echoes chasing its cry

it's a pen blossoming in lost hope
it's a blossom resisting the inevitable route

it's love's gleam waking to
light up landscape over zero

(David Hinton and Yanbing Chen)

Gains

A single mosquito
has enlarged night's size
taking a drop of my blood

I am a mosquito
reduced by night's size
taking a drop
of night's blood

I am a sizeless
hovering night
taking a drop
of heaven's blood

(Bonnie McDougall
and Chen Maiping)

The Bell

The bell tolls deep into autumn's hinterland
skirts scatter and fall on the trees
attempting to please the heavens

I watch the process of apples spoiling

children with a tendency to violence
ascend like black smoke
the roof tiles are damp

the three-mile storm has tireless masters

time's curtain
opened by the silent bellringer
disintegrates, adrift in the sky

the days strike, one endlessly after the other

boats land
sliding on the heavy snow
a sheep stares into the distance

its hollow gaze resembles peace

all things are being renamed
the ears of this mortal world
maintain a dangerous balance

– It rings a death knell

(Bonnie McDougall and Chen Maiping)

Sujata Bhatt

Indian □ 1956-

Born in Ahmedabad, Sujata Bhatt emigrated to the United States in her teens and now lives in Germany. A recipient of the Commonwealth Poetry Prize, she has published three volumes of verse, which have now been collected into one volume, *Point No Point* (Carcanet, 1997).

The One Who Goes Away

There are always, in each of us,
these two: the one who stays,
the one who goes away –

                              Eleanor Wilner

But I am the one
who always goes away.

The first time was the most –
was the most
        silent.
I did not speak,
did not answer
those who stood waving
with the soft noise
of saris flapping in the wind.

To help the journey
coconuts were flung
from Juhu beach
into the Arabian Sea –
But I saw beggars jump in
after those coconuts – a good catch
for dinner. And in the end
who gets the true luck
from those sacrificed coconuts?

I am the one
who always goes away.

Sometimes I'm asked if
I were searching for a place
that can keep my soul
from wandering
a place where I can stay
without wanting to leave.

Who knows.

Maybe the joy lies
in always being able to leave –

But I never left home.
I carried it away
with me – here in my darkness
in myself. If I go back, retrace my
                                    steps

I will not find
that first home anywhere outside
in that mother-land place.

We weren't allowed
    to take much
but I managed to hide
my home behind my heart.

Look at the deserted beach
now it's dusk – no sun
to turn the waves gold,
no moon to catch
the waves in silver mesh –

Look
at the in-between darkness
when the sea is unmasked
she's no beauty queen.
Now the wind stops
beating around the bush –

While the earth calls
and the hearth calls
come back, come back –

I am the one
who always goes away.

Because I must –

with my home intact
    but always changing
so the windows don't match
the doors anymore – the colours
clash in the garden –
And the ocean lives in the bedroom.

I am the one
who always goes
away with my home
which can only stay inside
in my blood – my home which
    does not fit
    with any geography.

The Langur Coloured Night

It was a cry
    to awaken the moon.

A sound to make the moon shout back.

It was the truth
    from a young langur.

It was a cry
      shining with moonlight,
a cry resounding against
white stone verandahs.

It was the langur
mirrored in that moon in the pond –
and the moon's face doubled
in the eyes of the langur.

It was the langur poised
                              grim-faced
                              stiff-haired
    between leaps.

It was a cry to breathe life
into the moon, the stones...

It was the langur
      just frozen, silver-jewelled with the moon.

It was the langur
      on his way to a tree.

It was a cry
      meant for no one
      but the moon – dear friend
of the langur who reveals the hiding places
of dogs, cats and even snakes.

It was the langur
      doing whatever he wanted to do

now that everyone is asleep.

What Happened to the Elephant?

What happened to the elephant,
the one whose head Shiva stole
to bring his son Ganesh
        back to life?

This is the child's curiosity
the nosy imagination that continues
probing, looking for a way
to believe the fantasy
a way to prolong the story.

If Ganesh could still be Ganesh
with an elephant's head,
then couldn't the body
        of that elephant
find another life
with a horse's head – for example?

And if we found
a horse's head to revive
the elephant's body –
Who is the true elephant?
And what shall we do
about the horse's body?

Still, the child refuses
to accept Shiva's carelessness
and searches for a solution
without death

*

But now when I gaze
at the framed postcard
of Ganesh on my wall,
I also picture a rotting carcass
of a beheaded elephant
        lying crumpled up
on its side, covered with bird shit
vulture shit –

Oh that elephant
        whose head survived
for Ganesh –

He died, of course, but the others
in his herd, the hundreds
in his family must have found him.
They stared at him for hours
with their slow swaying sadness...
How they turned and turned
in a circle, with their trunks
facing outwards and then inwards
towards the headless one.

That is a dance
        a group dance
no one talks about.

Muliebrity

I have thought so much about the girl
who gathered cow-dung in a wide, round basket
along the main road passing by our house
and the Radhavallabh temple in Maninagar.
I have thought so much about the way she
moved her hands and her waist
and the smell of cow-dung and road-dust and wet canna lilies,
the smell of monkey breath and freshly washed clothes
and the dust from crows' wings which smells different –
and again the smell of cow-dung as the girl scoops
it up, all these smells surrounding me separately
and simultaneously – I have thought so much
but have been unwilling to use her for a metaphor,
for a nice image – but most of all unwilling
to forget her or to explain to anyone the greatness
and the power glistening through her cheekbones
each time she found a particularly promising
mound of dung –

The Stare

There is that moment
when the young human child
stares
at the young monkey child
who stares back –

Innocence facing
innocence in a space
where the young monkey child
is not in captivity.

There is purity
   clarity

there is a transparence
   in this stare
which lasts a long time . . .

eyes of water
      eyes of sky
the soul can still fall through
because the monkey
has yet to learn fear –
and the human
has yet to learn fear
      let alone arrogance.

Witnessing it all
one can count eyelashes
one can count the snails
in the grass
    while waiting
for eyes to blink
waiting to see who
will look away first.

Still the monkey looks
at the human not in the same way
he would look at leaves
or at his own siblings.

And the human looks
at the monkey knowing
this is some totally other being.

And yet, there is such good will
such curiosity brightening
    their faces.

I would like to slip inside
that stare, to know
what the human child thinks
what the monkey child thinks
at that very moment.

Remember, the human child
is at that age
when he begins to use words
with power
but without the distance
of alphabets, of abstractions.

Mention bread
and he wants
a slice, buttered and with honey –
immediately.

Mention the cat
and he runs over
to awaken her.

The word
is the thing itself.

Language is simply
a necessary music
suddenly connected
    to the child's own heartbeat.

While the young monkey child
grows at a different rate,
looks at a tree, a bush,
at the human child
    and thinks.
Who knows what?

What remains burning
is that moment
of staring:
the two newly formed heads
balanced on fragile necks
tilting towards each other,
the monkey face
    and the human face
absorbing each other
with intense gentleness.

Oranges and Lemons

The second time
I came alone to say
a farewell of sorts, I wanted one more
look at her handwriting.

I was prepared for solitude, a floating
amputated quietness circling my wrists –
but not this song, not this

Oranges and lemons
Sold for a penny
All the schoolgirls
Are so many . . .

They rush in breathless
climbing up behind me, ahead of me, up
the warehouse steep Dutch staircase
to Anne Frank's room.

Schoolgirls, mostly schoolgirls
ages 13-16, they whisper about the important
things – staring everywhere: at windows, corners,
the ceiling. Staring at the paper,
her patient paper, her brown ink.
And a few linger behind, preferring to squint through
the netting, as if expecting something to happen
down by the other houses, the trees –

The grass is green
The rose is red
Remember me
when I am dead . . .

And a few linger behind,
whispering about the important things.

Wine from Bordeaux

Today I've invented a man
who has bought two thousand bottles
of a 1985 wine from Bordeaux,
the Bois-Malot which won
the Bronze Medal in 1986.
And now this 1985 Bois-Malot has become
even better than gold, and it will stay
good, it will delight you
        for years to come.

Over here, in Ostertor
you and I would have to pay
about *vierzehn Mark* for a bottle.
But I'm sure my imaginary man
has worked out some special deal
with the shopkeepers, maybe even
with the people
        who planted the grapes.

He's bought two thousand bottles already
and plans to buy more.

1985 is the year
before Chernobyl.

He doesn't like
to ingest anything harvested
        in Europe after 1985.

'This wine goes very well
with New Zealand lamb,'
he confides to the wine shop owner.
'It's the only meat
I feel safe eating . . . ' he whispers.

No doubt
he's got a large cellar
to hoard all those bottles
of crimson Bordeaux
with their handsome brown labels.
I imagine him smiling
at their sharp dark winks –
      rows and rows of rounded shadows
each time he opens the door.

There's another man
I can tell you about.
He is real.
He got himself sterilized
in May 1986 when he was eighteen
because he was convinced
his chromosomes were damaged.
And he didn't want to pass on
      any mistakes.

While the women
who gave birth over here
in 1986 sometimes didn't know
      what to eat.

I imagine some of them still
scrutinize their children
with fear, wishing they could supervise
the health of every cell.

While in the towns near Chernobyl
embryos didn't make it
fetuses didn't make it
and the babies who managed
to get born and who managed to grow
into children – suddenly
become sick with leukemia.

But the child
that I still think of
was one eight-year-old boy
who loved playing in the sand
      like most children
who didn't notice dirt or mud on his clothes
      like most children –

But then he started begging
to be allowed to take a shower
whenever he came indoors
thinking the water
      thinking the water would wash
           it all off–

Orpheus Confesses to Eurydice

1

It was a lack of faith.
I admit it. I didn't believe enough
in you or even in the power
of my song. I needed constant reassurance.
Yes, I saw how the Furies wept
as I sang slower, softer – Time stopped for me –
still, I didn't think they'd let you go.
I didn't think you'd be free to follow me.
And so I looked back
wondering: *were you really there?*

I've caught the snake
that killed you – I keep him
alive. He's become a sort of pet –
such a small viper, and so supple –

my last connection to you. And his brightness:
eyes, skin – how he shimmers in the sun – keeps me alert
and reminds me at times of your brightness:
the sun in your hair, the jewels around your neck.

At first, of course, I thought of revenge.
I thought of hurting the snake,
     of throwing him into a fire.
But I hesitated and now I've grown fond of him.

2

Once when I stood singing by the cliffs
a sharp stone fell – and then a lizard
darted to the east and her sliced-off tail
rushed away to the west – and I watched
the tail shudder and jerk –
a yellow-green thing in such a hurry.

Now I've become a torn-off
lizard's tail. Only my tongue lives
in my bodiless head – my tongue still sings
against the noise of the river.

Maybe this is what I really wanted:
To be just a tongue –
a lizard's tail without the lizard.

To be a pure voice
without my tired, awkward body –

Now I'm almost weightless and about to be swallowed
by the ocean – I will become
          a stronger voice.

Nina Cassian

Romanian – 1924-

A noted composer of chamber and symphonic music as well as of poetry, Nina Cassian has had to struggle throughout most of her creative life against political repression. When her early poems were condemned by the Stalinists (Romania was under Russian domination), for a while she concentrated on music; musical notes, she said, could not be found in the dictionary and therefore she could not be accused of making political references in her music. (Such a defence did not save Russian composers like Prokofiev from condemnation by Stalin.) After the death of Stalin there was a thaw and she published poetry again, but later censorship returned under the dictatorship of Ceausescu. In such an atmosphere, Nina Cassian's published verse concentrated on personal themes – love, death, loss, suffering – but she did circulate among her friends some satirical verses about the regime. When she was visiting New York in 1985, one of those friends was arrested, and copies of the verses were discovered at his house. The friend was tortured and finally killed; Cassian's house was ransacked and her books were banned. Thus she was forced into exile until Ceausescu fell from power. Many of the poems in her most recent collection, *Take My Word For It* (Anvil Press Poetry, 1998), were written in English.

Evolution

Today a grandly furious storm
hurled a pile of mussels at my feet,
reminding me of the first creation.
O sea, that element in which I was born.

Cradle of life, long convoy
of sea anemones, reptiles
and scaly monsters, winding toward us
imprisoned in our sweet and fragile forms . . .

I came from the sea and to the sea
I would return, to be immersed in her story,
ever lost and everlasting.
Black mussels on the shore: memento mori.

Greed

I am greedy. Puritans scold me
for running breathlessly
over life's table of contents
and for wishing and longing for everything.

They scold me for feasting
on joy and despair, together
with jugs of sour cream
and hot polenta.

They object to my wearing a tie pin
and a carnation in my hair,
for being sometimes boy, sometimes girl.
And who knows what else!

They rebuke me for not distributing love
according to a plan, for not rationing it,
for having a potter's agile hands
and now and then solving equations.

Well, that's my way! I'm hungry, I'm thirsty,
I rush through the world like a living sound.
I refuse to walk slowly, to crawl,
or to remain indebted for a kiss.

I'm greedy, I gulp things down, I fly,
and I'm proud that on my small lapel
occasionally a decoration glitters –
call it rapture, that golden rosette.

(Stanley Kunitz)

Longing

Oh my love
heavy anchor
hold me tight:
everything hurts,
mouth – from longing,
eyes – from light.

Winds have dropped –
maybe not,
but in the skies
silence reigns,
powerless
heaven sighs.

No more dreams
of steps in snow,
of foxes' traces,
no more flowers –
their hidden souls
sleep in bulbs.

Void. Loneliness . . .
Search is pointless –
all that is true
are my doubts:
How real are you?
How real were you?

(Brenda Walker and Andrea Deletant)

Pain

God, how they shrieked,
how they sobbed
the night birds.
God, how they cackled!
Wide-eyed,
I stared into the dark,
and on every rooftop,
the sea birds
clacked their beaks.
What an orgy of laughter!
The cold jeers
searched for me
in the solitude.
God, how they cackled,
strange city dwellers,
the night birds.
This is pain,
I told myself, keeping vigil.
This is how it hurts.
Deafening
silver wings,
voices, beaks, claws,
long knives in the night,
beaks by the window . . .
. . . you were far
our love over.

(Laura Schiff)

I Wanted to Stay in September

I wanted to stay in September
on that pale deserted beach.
I wanted to cram myself
with ashes from my unfaithful cranes
and let the slow, heavy wind
fall asleep in my long hair
like water in the trawl:
One night I wanted to light
a cigarette, whiter than the moon,
with no one around – just the sea
with its solemn, hidden force;
I wanted to stay in September,
witnessing the passage of time,
with one hand in the trees – the other
in the graying sand, to slip
along with summer into autumn . . .

But it seems my fate's cast
for more dramatic exist,
fated to be uprooted from landscapes
with an unprepared soul,
as I'm fated to quit loving
while still hired to love.

(Brenda Walker and Andrea Deletant)

Escape

He locked me in: his love – a prison.
His words and looks – padlocks.
I became blind and mute,
could no longer tell
a curtain from a river;
ashen grass, dead hair invaded me,
dead nails grew on my fingers,
a bluish skin covered my eyes.
I could no longer tell
a bracelet from a muzzle,
a wagon from a cello,
I was speechless – couldn't even answer
the call of the pomegranate seed,
or that kind invitation of frogs in the sunset
I wasn't even able to say "hello,"
– I lost a lot of friends.

Then suddenly, I noticed
my cheeks had become hollow to the touch
my hands uneven,
the body was entering its sheath
– and, realizing all this, with the speed of disgust
I cut off the dead nails,
excoriated my artificial eyes,
broke the lock
and ran out.
There was no guard.
No one to raise the alarm.
No one called out after me.
No one begged me to return.
Not a soul greeted me.
No one.

(Brenda Walker And Andrea Deletant)

The Young Bat

To begin, he circled my neck shyly
and laced it with his singing;
I almost fell in love with his ugly
triangular head, his squinting eyes,
and the sound of his frail bones.

At his first bite
I felt a great relief.
My pulse throbbed eagerly
knowing my blood would flow, diluted,
into another goitre, absolved of sin.

Then I grew weaker.
Clamped to my neck, the vampire
was drinking me, drinking me constantly.
His wings flared wide and free,
his eyes burned like two hieroglyphs–
but I couldn't decipher the message.

(Christopher Hewitt)

The Couple

Necks crossed, then parallel,
they float in slow motion
white and hazel
mingling their blond contrasts,
their floating heads
watching the world from lunar
          heights,
their fragile legs like antennae,
the bones of their foreheads
breathing sadness and exile
as they circle in their dismal arena,
straining upward to escape
as if pulled by invisible leashes
in love with their heads
but hating their captive bodies.
They separate, they follow
like the languid hours
of the final days
of an extinct species –
giraffes.

(Christopher Hewitt)

Ballad of the Jack of Diamonds

Here is the Jack of Diamonds, clad
In the rusty coat he's always had,
His two dark brothers wish him dead,
As does the third, whose hue is red.

Here is the Jack of Diamonds, whom
The fates have marked for certain doom.
He is a mediocre fellow,
A scrawny jack whose chest is hollow
And spattered with a dismal yellow –
No model for a Donatello.

The two dark brothers of this jack,
Abetted by the third, alack,
(Who, draped in hearts from head to foot,
Is the most knavish of the lot),
Have vowed by all means to be free
Of him who gives them symmetry,
Making a balanced set of four
Whose equilibrium they abhor.

One brother, on his breast and sleeves,
Is decked with tragic, spadelike leaves.
The next has crosses for décor.
The motif of the third is gore.

The Jack of Diamonds is dead,
Leaving a vacuum in his stead.

This ballad seems at least twice-told.
Well, all Romanian plots are old.

(Richard Wilbur)

Ars Poetica – A Polemic

I am I.
I am personal.
I am subjective, intimate, private,
                     particular,
confessional.
All that happens
happens to me.
The landscape I describe
is myself . . .

If you're interested
in birds, trees, rivers,
try reference books,
don't read my poems.
I'm no indexed bird,
tree or river,
just a registered Self.

                     (Nina Cassian and Brenda Walker)

Snowbound

I wear white handcuffs,
cold casts on my legs,
a white noose around my neck.

People go by in light outfits,
colourful birds painted on their shirts,
they yell at me to step aside,
call me a disgraceful invalid.
I can't reply.
My tongue is a frozen fish.

I'm besieged by a personal winter.
Nobody else seems to experience this rigidity, frigidity,
this stiff verticality of mine,
so inappropriate
in this surrounding, swarming, flexible, frantic world...

                     (Written in English)

Charles Causley

English – 1917-

Apart from six years in the navy during the Second World War, Charles Causley has lived all his life in Cornwall. His first book of poems was published in 1951, and since then his output has been prolific, making him one of Britain's most popular poets. The simplicity of Causley's language should not mislead the reader into thinking that his poems lack profundity of thought and feeling. Much of his poetry has been written in the ballad form; like W H Auden before him, he has celebrated "the ancient virtues of this particular kind of writing", which, he claims, keeps the writer from moralising while allowing "the incidents of his story to speak for themselves; and as we listen, we remain watchful for all kinds of ironic understatements".

Lord Sycamore

I climbed Lord Sycamore's castle,
   The wind was blowing red.
'Top of the morning, my lord,' I cried.
   'Top to you,' he said.

'Welcome to Sycamore Castle,'
   His smile as sharp as tin,
'Where many broken men come out
That in one piece go in.'

With pusser's eggs and bacon
   My belly it was rare.
'Together,' said Lord Sycamore,
'Let's take the dancing air.'

With a running finger
   He chucked me under the chin.

Felt with a lover's quiet hand
   Where he might best begin.

Suddenly he cooled me
   As we laughed and joked.
Although the month was May, my breath
   On the morning smoked.

On the sum of my body
   Lord Sycamore got to work,
Pulled the answer like a rose
   Out of my mouth with a jerk.

On Lord Sycamore's castle
   I heard the morning stop;
Over my head, the springing birds,
   Under my feet, the drop.

Recruiting Drive

Under the willow the willow
    I heard the butcher-bird sing,
Come out you fine young fellow
    From under your mother's wing.
I'll show you the magic garden
    That hangs in the beamy air,
The way of the lynx and the angry Sphinx
    And the fun of the freezing fair.

Lie down lie down with my daughter
    Beneath the Arabian tree,
Gaze on your face in the water
    Forget the scribbling sea.
Your pillow the nine bright shiners
    Your bed the spilling sand,
But the terrible toy of my lily-white boy
    Is the gun in his innocent hand.

You must take off your clothes for the doctor
    And stand as straight as a pin,
His hand of stone on your white breast-bone
    Where the bullets all go in.
They'll dress you in lawn and linen
    And fill you with Plymouth gin,
O the devil may wear a rose in his hair
    I'll wear my fine doe-skin.

My mother weeps as I leave her
    But I tell her it won't be long,
The murderers wail in Wandsworth Gaol
    But I shoot a more popular song.
Down in the enemy country
    Under the enemy tree
There lies a lad whose heart has gone bad
    Waiting for me, for me.

He says I have no culture
   And that when I've stormed the pass
I shall fall on the farm with a smoking arm
   And ravish his bonny lass.
Under the willow the willow
   Death spreads her dripping wings
And caught in the snare of the bleeding air
   The butcher-bird sings, sings, sings.

Ballad Of The Bread Man

Mary stood in the kitchen
   Baking a loaf of bread.
An angel flew in through the window.
   'We've a job for you,' he said.

'God in his big gold heaven,
   Sitting in his big blue chair,
Wanted a mother for his little son.
   Suddenly saw you there.'

Mary shook and trembled,
   'It isn't true what you say.'
'Don't say that,' said the angel
   'The baby's on its way.'

Joseph was in the workshop
   Planing a piece of wood.
'The old man's past it,' the neighbours said
   'That girl's been up to no good.'

'And who was that elegant fellow,
   They said, 'in the shiny gear?'
The things they said about Gabriel
   Were hardly fit to hear.

Mary never answered,
   Mary never replied.
She kept the information,
   Like the baby, safe inside.

It was election winter.
    They went to vote in town.
When Mary found her time had come
    The hotels let her down.

The baby was born in an annexe
    Next to the local pub.
At midnight, a delegation
    Turned up from the Farmers' Club.

They talked about an explosion
    That made a hole in the sky,
Said they'd been sent to the Lamb & Flag
    To see God come down from on high.

A few days later a bishop
    And a five-star general were seen
With the head of an African country
    In a bullet-proof limousine.

'We've come," they said, 'with tokens
    For the little boy to choose.'
Told the tale about war and peace
    In the television news.

After them came the soldiers
    With rifle and bomb and gun,
Looking for enemies of the state.
    The family had packed and gone.

When they got back to the village
    The neighbours said, to a man,
'That boy will never be one of us,
    Though he does what he blessed well can.'

He went round to all the people
    A paper crown on his head.
Here is some bread from my father.
    Take, eat, he said.

Nobody seemed very hungry.
    Nobody seemed to care.
Nobody saw the god in himself
    Quietly standing there.

He finished up in the papers.
    He came to a very bad end.
He was charged with bringing the living to life.
    No man was that prisoner's friend.

There's only one kind of punishment
    To fit that kind of a crime.
They rigged a trial and shot him dead.
    They were only just in time.

They lifted the young man by the leg,
    They lifted him by the arm,
They locked him in a cathedral
    In case he came to harm.

They stored him safe as water
    Under seven rocks.
One Sunday morning he burst out
    Like a jack-in-the-box.

Through the town he went walking.
    He showed them the holes in his head.
Now do you want any loaves? he cried.
    'Not today,' they said.

Ballad Of The Faithless Wife

    Carry her down to the river
        Carry her down to the sea
    Let the bully-boys stare at her braided hair
        But never a glance from me.

    Down by the writhing water
        Down by the innocent sand
    They laid my bride by the toiling tide
        A stone in her rifled hand.

Under the dainty eagle
   Under the ravening dove
Under a high and healthy sky
   I waited for my love.

Off she ran with a soldier
   Tall as a summer tree,
Soft as a mouse he came to my house
   And stole my love from me.

0 splintered were all the windows
   And broken all the chairs
War like a knife ran through my life
   And the blood ran down the stairs.

Loud on the singing morning
   I hear the mad birds rise
Safe from harm to the sun's alarm
   As the sound of fighting dies.

I would hang my harp on the branches
   And weep all through the day
But stranger, see! The wounded tree
   Has burned itself away.

False 0 false was my lover
   Dead on the diamond shore
White as a fleece, for her name wasPeace
   And the soldier's name was War.

The Question

In the locked sky beats a dove.
It speaks continually of love.

Deep in the river a talking stone
Says he lies easy who lies alone.

Under the stone there hides a knife:
The beginning and end of every life.

In the dark forest are flowers of light
That never fade by day or night.

Down in the valley stands a tree,
Its roots uneasy as the sea.

High on the tree there hangs a nest.
Here, says the wind, *you must take your rest.*

Through the spinney with eyes of wax
Runs the woodman with glaring axe.

Naked, my love and I arise
Bathed in his fearful prophecies.

Whose is the bird and whose the stone,
Whose is the light on the midnight sown?

Whose is the tree and whose the rest,
And whose is the knife upon my breast?

Who is the woodman and what does he cry?
Gaze in the mirror. Do not reply.

At The British War Cemetery, Bayeux

I walked where in their talking graves
And shirts of earth five thousand lay,
When history with ten feasts of fire
Had eaten the red air away.

'I am Christ's boy,' I cried, 'I bear
In iron hands the bread, the fishes.
I hang with honey and with rose
This tidy wreck of all your wishes.

'On your geometry of sleep
The chestnut and the fir-tree fly,
And lavender and marguerite
Forge with their flowers an English sky.

'Turn now towards the belling town
Your jigsaws of impossible bone,
And rising read your rank of snow
Accurate as death upon the stone.'

About your easy heads my prayers
I said with syllables of clay.
'What gift,' I asked, 'shall I bring now
Before I weep and walk away?'

Take, they replied, *the oak and laurel.*
Take our fortune of tears and live
Like a spendthrift lover. All we ask
Is the one gift you cannot give.

I Am The Great Sun
From a Normandy crucifix of 1632

I am the great sun, but you do not see me,
   I am your husband, but you turn away.
I am the captive, but you do not free me,
   I am the captain you will not obey.

I am the truth, but you will not believe me,
   I am the city where you will not stay,
I am your wife, your child, but you will leave me,
   I am that God to whom you will not pray.

I am your counsel, but you do not hear me,
   I am the lover whom you will betray,
I am the victor, but you do not cheer me,
   I am the holy dove whom you will slay.

I am your life, but if you will not name me,
Seal up your soul with tears, and never blame me.

Carol Ann Duffy

Scottish □ 1955□

Carol Ann Duffy was born in Glasgow, but has lived most of her life in England. Regarded by many as the outstanding poet of her generation in the United Kingdom, she has won many awards, including the Dylan Thomas Award and the Somerset Maugham Award. Her topics range from the personal to the social and political; she has a particular skill in the dramatic monologue, as is shown here in What Price? and Head of English.

What Price?

These were his diaries. Through the writing we may find
the man and whether he has been misjudged.
Admit it, even now, most people secretly resent
the Jews. We have all evening to peruse
the truth. Outside the window summer blossom falls.

It takes me back. I always saw some sense
in what he tried to do. This country should be strong.
I'll put some Wagner on the gramophone
then we can settle down. On nights like this
it makes one glad to be alive. My own Lili Marlene.

Of course, one had to fight. I had a wife.
But somewhere here I think you'll find
that he'd have joined with us. More wine?
I know the Sons of David died, some say atrociously,
but that's all past. The roses are in bloom.

Look at the way we claimed the islands back.
My grandchildren are young and pink
and make me proud. She has the right idea.
These journals will be his chance to explain,
I'm certainly convinced that they are real.

Not that he didn't make mistakes, but we can learn
from him. See by the larch tree how the sun goes down.

And notice all the interest from newspapers, so soon!
I admit that it was hell to be a Jew, but how much
do you think they'll fetch? One million? Two?

Head Of English

Today we have a poet in the class.
A real live poet with a published book.
Notice the inkstained fingers girls. Perhaps
we're going to witness verse hot from the press.
Who knows. Please show your appreciation
by clapping. Not too loud. Now

sit up straight and listen. Remember
the lesson on assonance, for not all poems,
sadly, rhyme these days. Still. Never mind.
Whispering's, as always, out of bounds –
but do feel free to raise some questions.
After all, we're paying forty pounds.

Those of you with English Second Language
see me after break. We're fortunate
to have this person in our midst.
Season of mists and so on and so forth.
I've written quite a bit of poetry myself,
am doing Kipling with the Lower Fourth.

Right. That's enough from me. On with the Muse.
Open a window at the back. We don't
want winds of change about the place.
Take notes, but don't write reams. Just an essay
on the poet's themes. Fine. Off we go.
Convince us that there's something we don't know.

Well. Really. Run along now girls. I'm sure
that gave an insight to an outside view.
Applause will do. Thank you
very much for coming here today. Lunch
in the hall? Do hang about. Unfortunately
I have to dash. Tracey will show you out.

Never Go Back

In the bar where the living dead drink all day
and a jukebox reminisces in a cracked voice
there is nothing to say. You talk for hours
in agreed motifs, anecdotes shuffled and dealt
from a well-thumbed pack, snapshots. The smoky mirrors
flatter; your ghost buys a round for the parched,
old faces of the past. Never return
to the space where you left time pining till it died.

Outside, the streets tear litter in their thin hands,
a tired wind whistles through the blackened stumps of houses
at a limping dog. *God, this is an awful place*
says the friend, the alcoholic, whose head is a negative
of itself. You listen and nod, bereaved. Baby,
what you owe to this place is unpayable
in the only currency you have. So drink up. Shut up,
then get them in again. Again. And never go back.

* * *

The house where you were one of the brides
has cancer. It prefers to be left alone
nursing its growth and cracks, each groan and creak
accusing as you climb the stairs to the bedroom
and draw your loved body on blurred air
with the simple power of loss. All the lies
told here and all the cries of love,
suddenly swarm in the room, sting you, disappear.

You shouldn't be here. You follow your shadow
through the house, discover that objects held
in the hands can fill a room with pain.
You lived here only to stand here now
and half-believe that you did. A small moment
of death by a window myopic with rain.
You learn this lesson hard, speechless, slamming
the front door, shaking plaster confetti from your hair.

* * *

A taxi implying a hearse takes you slowly,
the long way round, to the station. The driver
looks like death. The places you knew
have changed their names by neon, cheap tricks
in a theme-park with no theme. Sly sums of money
wink at you in the cab. At a red light,
you wipe a slick of cold sweat from the glass
for a drenched whore to stare you full in the face.

You pay to get out, pass the *Welcome To* sign
on the way to the barrier, an emigrant
for the last time. The train sighs
and pulls you away, rewinding the city like a film,
snapping it off at the river. You go for a drink,
released by a journey into nowhere, nowhen,
and all the way home you forget. Forget. Already
the fires and lights come on wherever you live.

Close

Lock the door. In the dark journey of our night,
two childhoods stand in the corner of the bedroom
watching the way we take each other to bits
to stare at our heart. I hear a story
told in sleep in a lost accent. You know the words.

Undress. A suitcase crammed with secrets
bursts in the wardrobe at the foot of the bed.
Dress again. Undress. You have me like a drawing,
erased, coloured in, untitled, signed by your tongue.
The name of a country written in red on my palm,

unreadable. I tell myself where I live now,
but you move in close till I shake, homeless,

further than that. A coin falls from the bedside table,
spinning its heads and tails. How the hell
can I win. How can I lose. Tell me again.

Love won't give in. It makes a hired room tremble
with the pity of bells, a cigarette smoke itself
next to a full glass of wine, time ache
into space, space, wants no more talk. Now
it has me where I want me, now you, you do.

Put out the light. Years stand outside on the street
looking up to an open window, black as our mouth
which utters its tuneless song. The ghosts of ourselves
behind and before us, throng in a mirror, blind,
laughing and weeping. They know who we are.

Originally

We came from our own country in a red room
which fell through the fields, our mother singing
our father's name to the turn of the wheels.
My brothers cried, one of them bawling *Home,
Home*, as the miles rushed back to the city,
the street, the house, the vacant rooms
where we didn't live any more. I stared
at the eyes of a blind toy, holding its paw.

All childhood is an emigration. Some are slow,
leaving you standing, resigned, up an avenue
where no one you know stays. Others are sudden.
Your accent wrong. Corners, which seem familiar,
leading to unimagined, pebble-dashed estates, big boys
eating worms and shouting words you don't understand.
My parents' anxiety stirred like a loose tooth
in my head. *I want our own country*, I said.

But then you forget, or don't recall, or change,
and, seeing your brother swallow a slug, feel only

a skelf of shame. I remember my tongue
shedding its skin like a snake, my voice
in the classroom sounding just like the rest. Do I only think
I lost a river, culture, speech, sense of first space
and the right place? Now, *Where do you come from?*
strangers ask. *Originally?* And I hesitate.

Yes, Officer

It was about the time of day you mention, yes.
I remember noticing the quality of light
beyond the bridge. I lit a cigarette.

I saw some birds. I knew the words for them
and their collective noun. A skein of geese. This cell
is further away from anywhere I've ever been. Perhaps.

I was in love. *For God's sake, don't.*
Fear is the first taste of blood in a dry mouth.
I have no alibi. Yes, I used to have a beard.

No, no. I wouldn't use that phrase. The more you ask
the less I have to say. There was a woman crying
on the towpath, dressed in grey. *Please. Sir.*

Without my own language, I am a blind man
in the wrong house. Here come the fists, the boots.
I curl in a corner, uttering empty vowels until

they have their truth. That is my full name.
With my good arm I sign a forgery. Yes, Officer,
I did. I did and these, your words, admit it.

Selling Manhattan

All yours, Injun, twenty-four bucks' worth of glass beads,
gaudy cloth. I got myself a bargain. I brandish
fire-arms and fire-water. Praise the Lord.
Now get your red ass out of here.

I wonder if the ground has anything to say.
You have made me drunk, drowned out
the world's slow truth with rapid lies.
But today I hear again and plainly see. Wherever
you have touched the earth, the earth is sore.

I wonder if the spirit of the water has anything
to say. That you will poison it. That you
can no more own the rivers and the grass than own
the air. I sing with true love for the land;
dawn chant, the song of sunset, starlight psalm.

Trust your dreams. No good will come of this.
My heart is on the ground, as when my loved one
fell back in my arms and died. I have learned
the solemn laws of joy and sorrow, in the distance
between morning's frost and firefly's flash at night.

Man who fears death, how many acres do you need
to lengthen your shadow under the endless sky?
Last time, this moment, now, a boy feels his freedom
vanish, like the salmon going mysteriously
out to sea. Loss holds the silence of great stones.

I will live in the ghost of grasshopper and buffalo.

The evening trembles and is sad.
A little shadow runs across the grass
and disappears into the darkening pines.

Nostalgia

Those early mercenaries, it made them ill –
leaving the mountains, leaving the high, fine air
to go down, down. What they got
was money, dull crude coins clenched
in the teeth; strange food, the wrong taste,
stones in the belly; and the wrong sounds,
the wrong smells, the wrong light, every breath –
wrong. They had an ache *here*, Doctor,
they pined, wept, grown men. It was killing them.

It was given a name. Hearing tell of it,
there were those who stayed put, fearful
of a sweet pain in the heart; of how it hurt,
in that heavier air, to hear
the music of home – the sad pipes – summoning,
in the dwindling light of the plains,
a particular place – where maybe you met a girl,
or searched for a yellow ball in long grass,
found it just as your mother called you in.

But the word was out. Some would never
fall in love had they not heard of love.
So the priest stood at the stile with his head
in his hands, crying at the workings of memory
through the colour of leaves, and the schoolteacher
opened a book to the scent of her youth, too late.
It was spring when one returned, with his life
in a sack on his back, to find the same street
with the same sign on the inn, the same bell
chiming the hour on the clock, and everything changed.

Odysseus Elytis
Greek – 1911-1995

Born in Crete, Elytis was educated in Athens and lived there for most of his life. In 1940-41 he was an officer in the Greek army resisting the invading Italians. In the post-war years his fame as a poet spread beyond Greece, and in 1979 he was awarded the Nobel Prize for literature.

Aegean

I

Love
The network of islands
And the prow of its foam
And the gulls of its dreams
On its highest mast a sailor
Whistles a song.

Love
Its song
And the horizons of its voyage
And the sound of its longing
On its wettest rock the bride
Waits for a ship.

Love
Its ship
And the nonchalance of its winds
And the jib sail of its hope
On the lightest of its waves an island
Cradles the arrival.

II

Playthings, the waters
In their shadowy flow
Speak with their kisses about the dawn
That begins
Horizoning –

And the pigeons in their cave
Rustle their wings
Blue awakening in the source
Of day
Sun –

The northwest wind bestows the sail
To the sea
The hair's caress
In the insouciance of its dream
Dew-cool –

Waves in the light
Revive the eyes
Where life sails towards

The recognition
Life –

      III

The surf a kiss on its caressed
         sand – Love
The gull bestows its blue liberty
To the horizon

Waves come and go
Foamy answer in the shell's ear.

Who carried away the blonde and
         sunburnt girl?
The sea-breeze with its
         transparent breath
Tilts dream's sail
Far out
Love murmurs its promise – Surf

         (Edmund Keeley and Philip Sherrard)

from The Gloria

    PRAISED BE the wooden table
the blond wine with the sun's stain
    the water doodling across the ceiling
the philodendron on duty in the corner

    The walls hand in hand with the waves
a foot that gathered wisdom in the sand
    a cicada that convinced a thousand others
conscience radiant like a summer

    PRAISED BE the heatwave hatching
the beautiful boulders under the bridge
    the shit of children with its green flies
a sea boiling and no end to it

    The sixteen deckhands hauling the net
the restless seagull slowly cruising
    stray voices out of the wilderness
a shadow's crossing through the wall

    THE ISLANDS with all their minium and lampblack
the islands with the vertebra of some Zeus

    the islands with their boat yards so deserted
the islands with their drinkable blue volcanoes

    Facing the meltemi with jib close–hauled
Riding the southwester on a reach
    the full length of them covered with foam
with dark blue pebbles and heliotropes

      Sifnos, Amorgos, Alonnisos
    Thasos, Ithaka, Santorini
       Kos, Ios, Sikinos

    PRAISED BE Myrto standing
on the stone parapet facing the sea
    like a beautiful eight or a clay pitcher
holding a straw hat in her hand

    The white and porous middle of day
the down of sleep lightly ascending
    the faded gold inside the arcades
and the red horse breaking free

    Hera of the tree's ancient trunk
the vast laurel grove, the light–devouring
    a house like an anchor down in the depths
and Kyra-Penelope twisting her spindle

    The straits for birds from the opposite shore
a citron from which the sky spilled out
    the blue hearing half under the sea
the long-shadowed whispering of nymphs and maples

    PRAISED BE, on the remembrance day
of the holy martyrs Cyricus and Julitta,
    a miracle burning threshing floors in the heavens
priests and birds chanting the *Ave*:

    HAIL, Girl Burning and hail Girl Verdant
Hail Girl Unrepenting, with the prow's sword

Hail you who walk and the footprints vanish
Hail you who wake and the miracles are born

Hail O Wild One of the depths' paradise
Hail O Holy One of the islands' wilderness

Hail Mother of Dreams, Girl of the Open Seas
Hail O Anchor-bearer, Girl of the Five Stars

Hail you of the flowing hair, gilding the wind
Hail you of the lovely voice, tamer of demons

Hail you who ordain the Monthly Ritual of the Gardens
Hail you who fasten the Serpent's belt of stars

Hail O Girl of the just and modest sword
Hail O Girl prophetic and daedalic

(Edmund Keeley and George Savidis)

The Sleep Of The Brave

They still smell of incense, and their faces are burnt by their crossing through the Great Dark Places.

There where they were suddenly flung by the Immovable

Face-down, on ground whose smallest anemone would suffice to turn the air of Hades bitter

(One arm outstretched, as though straining to be grasped by the future, the other arm under the desolate head, turned on its side,

As though to see for the last time, in the eyes of a disembowelled horse, the heap of smoking ruins) –

There time released them. One wing, the redder of the two, covered the world, while the other, delicate, already moved through space,

No wrinkle or pang of conscience, but at a great depth

The old immemorial blood that began painfully to etch, in the sky's blackness,

A new sun, not yet ripe,

That couldn't manage to dislodge the hoarfrost of lambs from live clover, but, before even casting a ray, could divine the oracles of Erebus ...

And from the beginning, Valleys, Mountains, Trees, Rivers,

A creation made of vindicated feelings now shone, identical and reversed, there for them to cross now, with the Executioner inside them put to death,

Villagers of the limitless blue:

Neither twelve o'clock striking in the depths nor the voice of the pole falling from the heights retracted their footsteps.

They read the world greedily with eyes now open forever, there where they were suddenly flung by the Immovable,

Face-down, and where the vultures fell upon them violently to enjoy the clay of their guts and their blood.

(Edmund Keeley and Philip Sherrard)

"With What Stones, What Blood, and What Iron..."

With what stones, what blood, and what iron,
With what fire are we made
Though we seem pure mist
And they stone us and say
That we walk with our heads in the clouds
How we pass our days and nights
God only knows

My friend, when night wakens your electric grief
I see the tree of the heart spreading
Your arms open beneath a pure Idea
To which you call
But which will not descend
For years and years:
It up there, and you down here

And yet longing's vision awakens flesh one day
And there where only bare solitude once shone
A city now laughs lovely as you would have it
You almost see it, it is waiting for you
Give me your hand so that we may go there before the Dawn
Floods it with cries of triumph
Give me your hand—before birds gather
On the shoulders of men to announce in song
That Virginal Hope is seen coming at last
Out of the distant sea.

We will go together, and let them stone us
And let them say we walk with our heads in the clouds —
Those who have never felt, my friend,
With what iron, what stones, what blood, what fire,
We build, dream, and sing.

(Edmund Keeley and Philip Sherrard)

"All Day Long We Walked In The Fields..."

All day long we walked in the fields
With our women, sons, and dogs
We played, sang, drank water
Fresh as it sprang from the ages

In the afternoon we sat for a moment
And we looked deeply into each other's eyes
A butterfly flew from our hearts
It was whiter
Than the small white branch at the tip of our dreams
We knew that it was never to disappear
That it did not remember at all what worms it bore

At night we lit a fire
And round about it sang:

Fire, lovely fire, do not pity the logs
Fire, lovely fire, do not turn to ash
Fire, lovely fire, burn us
                tell us of life.

We tell of life, we take it by the hands
We look into its eyes and it returns our look
And if this which makes us drunk is a magnet, we know it
And if this which gives us pain is bad, we have felt it

We tell of life, we go ahead
And say farewell to its birds, which are migrating

We are of a good generation.

                              (Edmund Keeley and Philip Sherrard)

The Mad Mad Boat
A Song

A ship decked with flags sails over the mountains
    and it starts manoeuvring: Heave-ho

It drops anchor among the pine trees
    it loads up with fresh air on both sides

It is made of black stone and of dream
    And it has an innocent boatswain and a cunning sailor

It comes out of the depths of old times
    It unloads sufferings and sighs

Christ, my Lord, I say it and I wonder
    at this mad mad boat this crazy ship

We've sailed on it for years and we haven't sunk yet
    One thousand captains we've changed

We were never afraid of cataclysms
    We entered everywhere and we went through everything

And we have on our mast an eternal
    sentinel, the Sun the Sovereign Sun!

U A Fanthorpe

English – 1929-

Ursula Fanthorpe was an English teacher for many years, but found that the demands of the job gave her little or no time for writing. She therefore left teaching to take a nine-to-five position as a clerk in a hospital in Bristol. Her experiences there provided her with the material for several of her poems. Her range is great: poems dealing with the small tragedies of ordinary life alternate with biting satire and sparkling wit. A study of U A Fanthorpe's work, *Taking Stock*, by Eddie Wainwright (Peterloo Poets) was published in 1995.

Casehistory: Alison (head injury)

(She looks at her photograph)

I would like to have known
My husband's wife, my mother's only daughter.
A bright girl she was.

Enmeshed in comforting
Fat, I wonder at her delicate angles.
Her autocratic knee

Like a Degas dancer's
Adjusts to the observer with airy poise,
That now lugs me upstairs

Hardly. Her face, broken
By nothing sharper than smiles, holds in its smiles
What I have forgotten.

She knows my father's dead,
And grieves for it, and smiles. She has digested
Mourning. Her smile shows it.

I, who need reminding
Every morning, shall never get over what
I do not remember.

Consistency matters.
I should like to keep faith with her lack of faith,
But forget her reasons.

Proud of this younger self,
I assert her achievements, her A levels,
Her job with a future.

Poor clever girl! I know,
For all my damaged brain, something she doesn't:
I am her future.

A bright girl she was.

Reports

Has made a sound beginning
Strikes the right note:
Encouraging, but dull.
Don't give them anything
To take hold of. Even
Pronouns are dangerous.

The good have no history,
So don't bother. *Satisfactory*
Should satisfy them.

Fair and *Quite good*,
Multi-purpose terms,
By meaning nothing,
Apply to all.
Feel free to deploy them.

Be on your guard;
Unmanageable oaf cuts both ways.
Finds the subject difficult,
Acquitting you, converts
Oaf into idiot, usher to master.

Parent, child, head,
Unholy trinity, will read
Your scripture backwards.
Set them no riddles, just
Echo the common-room cliché:
Must make more effort.

Remember your high calling:
School is the world.
Born at *Sound beginning,*
We move from *Satisfactory*

To *Fair*, then *Find*
The *subject difficult*,
Learning at last we
Could have done better.

Stone only, final instructor,
Modulates from the indicative
With *Rest in peace*.

BC:AD

This was the moment when Before
Turned into After, and the future's
Uninvented timekeepers presented arms.

This was the moment when nothing
Happened. Only dull peace
Sprawled boringly over the earth.

This was the moment when even energetic Romans
Could find nothing better to do
Than counting heads in remote provinces.

And this was the moment
When a few farm workers and three
Members of an obscure Persian sect

Walked haphazard by starlight straight
Into the kingdom of heaven.

You will be hearing from us shortly

You feel adequate to the demands of this position?
What qualities do you feel you
Personally have to offer?

                                          Ah

Let us consider your application form.
Your qualifications, though impressive, are
Not, we must admit, precisely what
We had in mind. Would you care
To defend their relevance?

  Indeed

Now your age. Perhaps you feel able
To make your own comment about that,
Too? We are conscious ourselves
Of the need for a candidate with precisely
The right degree of immaturity.

                                            So glad we agree

And now a delicate matter: your looks.
You do appreciate this work involves
Contact with the actual public? Might they,
Perhaps, find your appearance
Disturbing?

                                                    Quite so

And your accent. That is the way
You have always spoken, is it? What
Of your education? Were
You educated? We mean, of course,
Where were you educated?
                            And how
Much of a handicap is that to you,
Would you say?

                                        Married, children,
We see. The usual dubious
Desire to perpetuate what had better
Not have happened at all. We do not
Ask what domestic disasters shimmer
Behind that vaguely unsuitable address.

And you were born –?

                                                Yes. Pity.

So glad we agree.

Not My Best Side
(Uccello: S. George and the Dragon, The National Gallery)

I

Not my best side, I'm afraid.
The artist didn't give me a chance to
Pose properly, and as you can see,
Poor chap, he had this obsession with
Triangles, so he left off two of my
Feet. I didn't comment at the time
(What, after all, are two feet
To a monster?) but afterwards
I was sorry for the bad publicity.
Why, I said to myself, should my conqueror
Be so ostentatiously beardless, and ride
A horse with a deformed neck and square hoofs?
Why should my victim be so
Unattractive as to be inedible,
And why should she have me literally
On a string? I don't mind dying
Ritually, since I always rise again,
But I should have liked a little more blood
To show they were taking me seriously.

II

It's hard for a girl to be sure if
She wants to be rescued. I mean, I quite
Took to the dragon. It's nice to be
Liked, if you know what I mean. He was
So nicely physical, with his claws
And lovely green skin, and that sexy tail,
And the way he looked at me,
He made me feel he was all ready to
Eat me. And any girl enjoys that.
So when this boy turned up, wearing machinery,
On a really *dangerous* horse, to be honest,

I didn't much fancy him. I mean,
What was he like underneath the hardware?
He might have acne, blackheads or even
Bad breath for all I could tell, but the dragon –
Well, you could see all his equipment
At a glance. Still, what could I do?
The dragon got himself beaten by the boy,
And a girl's got to think of her future.

III

I have diplomas in Dragon
Management and Virgin Reclamation.
My horse is the latest model, with
Automatic transmission and built-in
Obsolescence. My spear is custom-built,
And my prototype armour
Still on the secret list. You can't
Do better than me at the moment.
I'm qualified and equipped to the
Eyebrow. So why be difficult?
Don't you want to be killed and/or rescued
In the most contemporary way? Don't
You want to carry out the roles
That sociology and myth have designed for you?
Don't you realize that, by being choosy,
You are endangering job-prospects
In the spear- and horse-building industries?
What, in any case, does it matter what
You want? You're in my way.

Sunderland Point and Ribchester

Sunderland Point, where sea, wind, sky
Dispute dominion, on a spur of land
So bitter that you'd think no one would take
The trouble to go there.
                              Here SAMBO lies,
A faithful NEGRO, who (attending his Mafter
From the Weft Indies) DIED
On his Arrival at Sunderland.
It is, of course, unconsecrated ground.

Now children stagger here on pilgrimage,
Their offerings the sort of things you'd find
On a pet's grave: a cross of driftwood, lashed
With binder-twine; a Woolworth vase,
Chocked up with grit and pebbles, crammed
With dead wild flowers.
                              Sam lies very low.
You can allow him any voice you like.
Despair, pneumonia, exile, love, are variously
Thought to have killed him. A good place
To bring the kids in summer at weekends.

Ribchester had a stone, now lost.
Camden preserved the proper idiom:
*By this earth is covered she who was once
Aelia Matrona, who lived 28 years, 2 months,
And 8 days, and Marcus Julius Maximus,
Her son, who lived 6 years, 3 months,
And 20 days.*
                        A place to bring the kids.

Children are the most authentic
Pilgrims, having farthest to go, and knowing
Least the way.
                The Romans understood
The use and pathos of arithmetic.
And the Ribble bites its banks, and the sea gnaws at the shore.
So many patterns gone, the *faithful slave*, the *son*
Most dutiful to his father. The word
Strives to be faithful, but the elements
Are against it.
                We are all exiles, Sam,
From the almost-forgotten country
Before the divorce, before the failed exam,
Before the accident, before the white man came.
Your situation's more extreme than most,
But we all of us, all of us seek
That country. And you, who so clearly were not
Your own man, lying in no man's land,
A journey's end for children, seem in your muteness
To be meaning something.
Alternative:
The massive Roman formulas: *the century*
Of Titius built 27 feet . . .
. . . *According to the reply of the god*.

Halley's Comet 1985-86

(in honour of Patrick Moore)
Written at the request of Cleone, Viscountess Parker, for her children,
Tanya, Katharine and Marian, descendants of George Parker,
2nd Earl of Macclesfield, astronomer, who was responsible
for Britain's adoption of the Gregorian calendar.

I am the long-haired athlete of the sky,
Always predictable, never quite precise.

Who lives to see me twice
Lives to be old.

Many kept vigil for me: Chinese astronomers
With their strong bare eyes; Harold
And his star-crossed Saxons, stitched
Into history deciphering disaster
From my tail; candid Giotto of the perfect circle
Showed me tacitly on fresco; and Kepler knew me,
Walking home at midnight from a party.

Men without telescopes or truthful clocks.

Then Halley named me and reckoned my route.

Heavenly eccentric, syncopating centuries,
I visit dearest Earth, so green and blue and small,
Looping my orbit round her hemispheres,
Springing past Sun to beyond-sight Neptune,
Slow and more slow, and lagging as I spin,
Then widdershins back, towards new techniques,
New signs of love. Earth shines more bright for me.

This time my lover sends me dancing-partners
Whom I shall shatter in my dusty unveiling.

For those I favour are the patient men
Who watch, who wait, show children where to find me.

Nativities

Godlings are born racily.

They are excavated
Into life by the strong licks
Of the world-cow, suckled
By goats, mares, wolves.

Blossom of oak, blossom of broom,
Blossom of meadowsweet
Go to their making.

They erupt through the paternal
Skull fully armed, hatch from an egg,
Or appear, foam-born,
In Cyprus, in a shell,
Wearing a great deal of hair
And nothing else.

This one arrived
At the time of the early lambs
By means of the usual channels.

Miroslav Holub

Czech □ 1923-1998

Miroslav Holub has been described by Ted Hughes as one of the half dozen most interesting poets writing anywhere. In his introduction to Holub's *On the Contrary* (1977), the English critic A Alvarez wrote:

> As a scientist, he has a solid international reputation; as a poet, his intelligence, wit and vulnerability, his clarity and unflagging distaste for whatever is pretentious or second-hand have made him one of the most original and certainly one of the sanest voices of our time.

Holub's education was solidly classical, and Homer and Virgil the first poets he studied. When he finished school in Nazi-occupied Czechoslovakia, he was put to work as a labourer on the railways; after the War he studied science and medicine at Charles University in Prague, eventually becoming a noted immunologist. In the political repression that followed the 'Prague Spring' of 1969 he became a 'non-person', and his work was suppressed in his home country; he himself, however, had managed to leave Czechoslovakia and find work first in the USA and then in Germany. Reviewing Holub's *Notes of a Clay Pigeon*, Douglas Sealy wrote:

> Holub views the world as a hitherto unexplored country; everything is strange and nothing can be taken for granted ...

Four of the six poems chosen here have been translated by different hands. Hence it has been possible to set two different versions side by side for comparison and analysis.

Brief reflection on accuracy

Fish
    always accurately know where to move and when,
    and likewise
    birds have an accurate built-in time sense
    and orientation.

Humanity, however,
    lacking such instincts resorts to scientific
    research. Its nature is illustrated by the following
    occurrence.

A certain soldier
    had to fire a cannon at six o'clock sharp every evening.
    Being a soldier he did so. When his accuracy was
    investigated he explained:

I go by
    the absolutely accurate chronometer in the window
    of the clockmaker down in the city. Every day at seventeen
    forty-five I set my watch by it and
    climb the hill where my cannon stands ready.
    At seventeen fifty-nine precisely I step up to the cannon
    and at eighteen hours sharp I fire.

And it was clear
    that this method of firing was absolutely accurate.
    All that was left was to check that chronometer. So
    the clockmaker down in the city was questioned about
    his instrument's accuracy.

Oh, said the clock maker,
    this is one of the most accurate instruments ever. Just imagine,
    for many years now a cannon has been fired at six o'clock sharp.
    And every day I look at this chronometer
    and always it shows exactly six.

So much for accuracy.
    And fish move in the water, and from the skies
    comes a rushing of wings while

Chronometers tick and cannon boom.   (Ewald Osers)

Brief Thoughts on Exactness

Fish
>move exactly there and exactly then,

just as
>birds have their inbuilt exact measure of time and place.

But mankind,
>deprived of instinct, is aided
>by scientific research, the essence of which
>this story shows.

A certain soldier
>had to fire a gun every evening exactly at six.
>He did it like a soldier. When his exactness
>was checked, he stated:

I follow
>an absolutely precise chronometer in the shop-window
>of the clockmaker downtown. Every day at seventeen
>forty-five I set my watch by it and
>proceed up the hill where the gun stands ready.
>At seventeen fifty-nine exactly I reach the gun
>and exactly at eighteen hours I fire.

It was found
>that this method of firing was absolutely exact.
>There was only the chronometer to be checked.
>The clockmaker downtown was asked about its exactness.

Oh, said the clockmaker,
>this instrument is one of the most exact. Imagine,
>for years a gun has been fired here at six exactly.
>And every day I look at the chronometer
>and it always shows exactly six.

So much for exactness.
>And the fish move in the waters and the heavens are filled
>with the murmur of wings, while

The chronometers tick and the guns thunder.

>>(Jarmila and Ian Milner)

Brief reflection on laughter

In laughter we stretch the mouth from ear to ear,
   or at least in that direction,
   we bare our teeth and in that way reveal
   long-past stages in evolution
   when laughter still was an expression of
   triumph over a slain neighbour.

We expel our breath right up from the throat,
   according to need we gently vibrate our
   vocal chords, if necessary we also touch our foreheads
   or the back of our heads, or we rub our hands or slap
   our thighs, and in that way reveal long-past stages
   when victory also presupposed
   fleetness of foot.

Generally speaking, we laugh when we feel like laughing.

In special instances we laugh
   when we don't feel like laughing at all,
   we laugh because laughter is prescribed or
   we laugh because it isn't prescribed.

And so, in effect, we laugh all the time, if only
to conceal the fact that all the time someone
is laughing at us.

(Ewald Osers)

Brief Thoughts on Laughter

When laughing we stretch the mouth from ear to ear,
    or at least in that direction,
    and bare the teeth, thereby indicating
    bygone stages of development
    when laughter expressed
    triumph over a fallen twin-brother.

We breathe out deeply from the throat,
    according to need, gently vibrate
    the vocal chords, or touch our forehead
    or nape, or rub our hands and slap
    our thighs, indicating the bygone stages
    when victory also presupposed
    swift legs.

Generally speaking, we laugh when we feel like it.

In special cases we laugh
    when we don't feel like it at all,
    we laugh because it is prescribed, or
    we laugh because it is not prescribed.

And in fact we laugh our heads off
    so that we won't hear how someone
    is laughing at us all the time.

                                                    (Jarmila and Ian Milner)

Brief Thoughts on a Test-Tube

You take
    a bit of fire, a bit of water,
    a bit of rabbit or tree,
    or any little piece of man,
    you mix it, shake well, cork it up,
    put it in a warm place, in darkness, in light, in frost,
    leave it alone for a while – though things don't leave you alone –
    and that's the whole point.

And then
    you have a look – and it grows,
    a little sea, a little volcano,
    a little tree, a little heart, a little brain,
    so small you don't hear it pleads
    to be let out,
    and that's the whole point, not to hear.

Then you go
    and record it, all the minuses or
    all the pluses, some with an exclamation–mark,
    all the zeros, or all the numbers, some with an exclamation–mark,
    and the point is that the test-tube
    is an instrument for changing question-
    into exclamation-marks,

And the point is
    that for the moment you forget
    you yourselves are

In the test-tube.

                                                  (Jarmila and Ian Milner)

Brief Reflection on Test-Tubes

Take
    a piece of fire, a piece of water,
    a piece of a rabbit or a piece of a tree,
    or any piece of a human being,
    mix it, shake it, stopper it up,
    keep it warm, in the dark, in the light, refrigerated,
    let it stand still for a while–yourselves far from still –
    but that's the real joke.

After a while
    you look – and it's growing,
    a little ocean, a little volcano,
    a little tree, a little heart, a little brain,
    so little you don't hear it lamenting
    as it wants to get out,
    but that's the real joke, not hearing it.

Then go
    and record it, all dashes or
    all crosses, some with exclamation-marks,
    all noughts and all figures, some with exclamation-marks
    and that's the real joke, in effect a test-tube
    is a device for changing noughts
    into exclamation-marks.

That's the real joke
    which makes you forget for a while
    that really you yourself are

    In the test-tube.

(Ewald Osers)

Minotaur's Thoughts on Poetry

It is certain that it exists. Because
on dark nights when I walk
unseen through the snail-winding streets
my own roaring echoes back
from afar.

Yes. It exists. We know that in former times
cicadas were of gigantic size
and even today one can find a mammoth's nest
under a pebble. The earth then
is lighter than before.

Moreover development is nothing else than
making a faux pas once again
and it does happen that a severed head
may sing.

And it isn't from the discovery of words
as many believe. Blood
in the corner of the mouth is essentially
more original and the gnashing of teeth
heats the nuclei of the rocky planets.

That it exists is certain.
Because
thousands of bulls want to be
people.
And vice versa.

(Jarmila and Ian Milner)

The Minotaur's thoughts on poetry

Certainly this thing exists. For
on dark nights when, unseen,
I walk through the snail-like windings of the street
the sound of my own roar reaches me
from a great distance.

Yes. This thing exists. For surely
even cicadas were once of gigantic stature
and today you can find mammoths' nests
under a pebble. The earth, of course,
is lighter than it once was.

Besides, evolution is nothing but
a long string of false steps;
and it may happen that a severed head
will sing.

And it's not due, as many believe, to
the invention of words. Blood
in the corners of the mouth is substantially
more ancient and the cores of the rocky planets
are heated by the grinding of teeth.

Certainly this thing exists.
Because
a thousand bulls want to be
human.
And vice versa.

(Ewald Osers)

The soul

In Queen's Street
on Friday night
– lights only just blossoming
but already with the pomegranates
of shows for adults only –
among the herds of cars
a yellow
inflatable balloon
was bouncing about
with what remained of its helium
soul,
still two lives left,

amidst the song of armour
bouncing with yellow
balloon fright

in front of wheels
and behind wheels,

incapable of salvation and
incapable of destruction,
one life left,
half a life left,
just a molecular trace of helium,

and with its last ounce of strength
searching with its string
for a small child's hands
on Sunday morning.

(Ewald Osers)

Swans in flight

It's like violence done to the atmosphere; as if Michelangelo reached out from the stone. And all the swans on the entire continent always take off together, for they are linked by a single signalling circuit. They are circling, and that means that Fortinbras's army is approaching. That Hamlet will be saved and that an extra act will be played. In all translations, in all theatres, behind all curtains and without mercy.

The actors are already growing wings against fate.

Hold out – that's all.

(Ewald Osers)

Ivan Lalić

Serbo-Croat □ 1931-1996

The leading poet of what was once Yugoslavia, Ivan Lalić was a Serb married to a Croat. Born in Belgrade in 1931, he published fourteen collections of poetry; a selection of his verse, translated by Francis Jones, was published in 1996 under the title *A Rusty Needle* (Anvil Press Poetry).

How Orpheus Sang

A thicket of song, with every note a rose;
A voice of copper, of fruit and foam; a space
Where every branch outstretches, lengthens and grows
All soft beneath the bark, as if to expose
Its blackened body to a woman's embrace.

The beasts of the field and forest scarcely sensed
The moment their blood congealed to mead. Yet here
They stand, the great with the small, all bristling, tensed;
Sculpted, it seems, where the silence has condensed,
A lake of light in every attentive ear.

In his singing, time is translated to sound,
Softened into the limpid, protean form
Of shallow water where red-dappled trout abound,
The speckled tints of flowered and grassy ground,
And the taste of sunlit soil, humid and warm.

And he sings his song in the gentle, pouring rain,
In the purple clover; the raw flesh pulsates
Under his skin; but his ears secretly strain
For a wiser voice to echo the refrain
Beneath the stone, where silence's first wave waits.

Ophelia

The rivers rock her as they bear
Her body, white and swollen with water;
They swirl her lush and unkempt hair
Braided with twigs where branches have caught her.

The depths are caressed by two soft hands:
Beneath them, minnows uneasily flit;
Her neck is wreathed with water-weed strands;
Like rotting cherries, her lips have split.

Inquisitive raindrops sometimes spill
Into each sky-blue, wide-open eye,
And trickle from her lids until
A drifting cloud sponges them dry.

Sometimes a wind in the rushes will chase
A wave across the water – it slips
Like rippling laughter over her face:
The river is learning to smile with her lips.

The current carries no empty shell,
No water-shadow, futile and blind,
For another seeks her beauty's spell:
With death himself she lies entwined.

This is sensed by the shrieking crows,
The hollow reeds, and frost's first ashes
Along the banks; is known to the snows,
Its early flakes impaled on her lashes.

Ophelia, why not try to weep;
Alive with death, to sink anew,
And free your dead love from his keep –
Or does he still mean freedom for you?

Slow your progress: bridges quiver,
Sails are bathed in the heat of the sun.

Death in your flesh, the gurgling river
Beneath you: is your suffering done?

Surely, Ophelia, you did no wrong:
You're only weak, so the waters bear
Your body, your arms dangling along,
Twigs entangled in your hair.

But once you decay you will be saved,
As death within you forgets his desire –
Then give way to the tears you've craved,
And sink like a star to the depths of the mire.

Requiem For A Mother

Licht: der Liebe! scheinest du denn auch Toten, du goldnes!
– Hölderlin

The winds clothe the sky over our city
And know nothing of poverty. But no winds
Ripple the mirrors of your dead eyes,
Halted, like a little flood, beneath the roots
Of a forked lime tree. Between you and the light
Lives earth. Look – you are walled into silence
Like a bird into light, together with the dead years,
Whose blood has clotted to berries of darkness
under the vault.

*I hear footsteps teeming like ants
And the flat fall of the leaves. Where is my boy,
With light's unfocused image in his inherited eyes?*

Shoots of grass have riddled the russet soil.
You lie unmoving, your voice plundered,
Full to the eyes with love under seal.
Did you recognise these steps, once a boy's,
Cut short at the edge of your silence
As fish hold back before a shore?
He leans against the forked lime tree,
Facing your name. Brimful of words, like a bell.

He has stopped. Those steps grew from me.
Is that my boy, who has come of age between the great
Shattered windows of the unknown years?

Sleep on, walled so solidly into your silence, and listen
As you sleep to the little lizards basking in the sun
And the sprouting of the grass. The man once a boy has said
With an inherited voice: the tongue of the name of my love
Lives in the things which encircle love.
If I am no better for this (though goodness flows
Like the tide in little coves), at least I am richer,
Like a tree which is forced to leaf.

My boy. My eyes, wiped clean of death.
Happy, he turns and walks away. My boy.

Of Eurydice

No one prevented me plunging my voice,
Plated in violet silver, into your darkness,
Your thick darkness devoid of time;
But my voice melted on your sweaty palms, choked
On black feathers from the strata of dead birds,
And vapourised on the coals of wisdom in your eyes,
And now, gnawed to the bone by the walls' invisible sneers,
I return alone.

Lords of the back of duration, had love
Not suffused my crimson fear, as the
South wind is drenched with the smell of the sea,
I would not have knocked at the doors of forbidden return.
But you let me tell the sands of dead time, and
Spattered me with your knowing, silent laughter
When I believed my blood-heavy eyes.

I was alone, you see. And I walked
Your corridors, only to stay so.
But still I robbed your darkness of a little light
And touched your tranquil lips and limbs,

To understand the senseless meaning of my loss.
Eurydice, unravelled like a tree into its roots,
Lasts on outside me, without a farewell wave.

And now, gnawed to the bone by the walls' invisible sneers,
I dig my nails into my dumbstruck, ashy palms,
To leave as I came, with dignity,
Not crying out, nor running for the doors of the sun,

Afraid, and hideously enriched.

From the cycle 'Orpheus on Deck'

Letter From The Knight Sinadin
who fell in the Battle of Angora in the Year of Our Lord 1402

We crossed the narrow neck of sea, blue, dancing,
And swam into stone, into sand mad with winds,
Into a sun without sky, strangers among strangers.
The sea, flowering in light and foam, stayed
On the other side, behind our hearts. We rode through
Weeks overgrown with the dark foliage of roads,
Rutted roads, the pain of hooves, and evenings
Which sucked the sun from our scorching armour.
O fate, how you are peopled with wonders!
Our enemy was unknown, as were the women
Whose smiles stayed melting on the tracery grilles
Of houses girdled by walls and silence, still
Unforgotten. But when the drumming doubled,
And when the dry earth went mad with fear,
We struck eyes eaten out by the wind:
Then we recognised the hatred in the future victors,
While our eyes were the great empty sky.
Why did we fill it with the blood and iron of arrows?
And now we retreat and close our ears
To hide the sound of the grass growing up like knives
On the sand of our graves.

Princip On The Battlefield
to my father

Emerging onto an empty field,
With no wedding ring, no coat of many colours,
No Blessed Prince's tent,

There was thunder last night, a short squall,
The scent of the limes richer for the short memory of lightning,

My hand against my forehead, this wind
Five centuries heavy, shimmering, huge,
The banner under which I stumble,

At a street corner with a view of the river,
Where time starts to sing in the voices of old men
Blind with black sun,

With no armour, I mingle between the passers-by
And the gilded shadows,
With no option now, I stand on a empty field
Where the hooves of battle pound.

I raise my hand:

– Let all be blessed and just –
And fire.

The Argonauts

The sea let us be, engrossed with the eternity
In herself; and so we sailed, from shore
To shore, for days, for nights, for years.

The loveliest shores, of course, we left untouched:
Except for unravelled threads of scent borne on the wind
From the vast orchards at the ends of the earth,

Beyond the path of our sailing; and yet
We learnt love, and death, and a little sense,
Hard grains of gold in the sand of memory;

Yes, and the pride of adventure, defiled with blood
And washed in the clean winds, beneath the stars
Where we clumsily wrote our names.

We came back, in the end, to where we began;
The crew scattered like a necklace: our destiny's thread
Had snapped. The captain crushed beneath the keel.

The sea was still the same. Everything was still the same.
The ship, her ribs blossomed open, lies rotting on the starting shore,
But few know the secret:
        the end does not matter,
What matters is only the sailing.

Young Woman From Pompeii

I curled up, shrinking like the pupil of an eye
Adapting too late to that cruel glare,
And fallen to earth, I rested my burnt forehead
On my arm.
        After that
My name disintegrated even faster
Than my tender flesh, in suffocating bitterness.
I forgot to count, to breathe,
And to look back. I was emptiness,
I was the dark cloud of my movement,
A bubble in a sea of dead fire. Thus
I awaited the slimy touch of wet clay
Filling me without passion, as water
Fills a footprint on deserted sands.

And what do you know of me now? Barely something
Of my brief wish to outlive myself,
Only a gesture, perhaps of weeping, and a shape
Sealed accidentally and in haste.
So how can I tell you that there exists
A domain where I am more real than the voice
Trying to imprison me, more solid

Than the light in which you look at me?
You think you know me? Go on,
Touch this shoulder: I am not there.
But my touch is much lighter:
                          there –
You are not who you were a moment ago. I know you
And burn on your shoulder, before the fire,
Before the ashes, before and after everything.

The Spaces of Hope

I have experienced the spaces of hope,
The spaces of a moderate mercy. Experienced
The places which suddenly set
Into a random form: a lilac garden,
A street in Florence, a morning room,
A sea smeared with silver before the storm,
Or a starless night lit only
By a book on the table. The spaces of hope
Are in time, not linked into
A system of miracles, nor into a unity;
They merely exist. As in Kanfanar,
At the station; wind in a wild vine
A quarter-century ago: one space of hope.
Another, set somewhere in the future,
Is already destroying the void around it,
Unclear but real. Probable.

In the spaces of hope light grows,
Free of charge, and voices are clearer,
Death has a beautiful shadow, the lilac blooms later,
But for that it looks like its first-ever flower.

Gwyneth Lewis

Welsh – 1959-

Gwyneth Lewis writes both in Welsh, her first language, and in English. She has published two volumes of verse in English, *Parables and Faxes* (Bloodaxe, 1995) and *Zero Gravity* (Bloodaxe, 1998).

Peripheral Vision

Not everyone sees it, but I glimpsed the man
inside our terrier. We'd walked up the lane,
he stood back, a second, to let me in

Through the gate, so courtly that, on my inner eye,
I saw him for the first time clearly
not a dog but a dish dressed in soft chamois,

tall like a prince, with thigh-length boots.
I said I would marry him. Sepia street lights
were our veil as, with love, I opened the locks

to our royal dwelling. Then, back on all fours,
he was wagging his tail by the kitchen door.
Beauty hides in the beast. This is the law.

Flyover Elegies
(For Jane)

I

The traffic's been worse than ever this year,
straining bumper to choking tail,
inching towards the roundabout. We feel
that there's less oxygen to breathe in air,

Less room for manoeuvre. Your flyover's arch
holds cars in a rainbow, its pot of gold
somewhere in town. Meanwhile, below,
mothers with pushchairs use the underpass,

Struggle with shopping. These are the circles
of Dante's hell. There's the view
from the parapet, of course. But you,
like the transport, wanted somewhere else.

II

I remember the flyover being built.
The word was for freedom, for rising high
and swiftly, for avoiding a wait.
It was for cruising, for a wider view,
it was for people just passing through.

It sounded like death. All day the pile-
drivers thudded into the earth
with a sickening heartbeat. Flying takes violence and, the thing is, cement
needs a body before it's a monument.

Fax X

Today set sail like a cruising ship
taking us with it, so we waved goodbye
to the selves that we were yesterday
and left them ashore like a memory
while we launched out on the open sea,
were travelling! The breeze grew stiff
so we grabbed the railings, tasted the surf
as the sky came towards us, the equator noon
a place to pass us, while the tropics of tea
swung over us and straight on by
as time kept sailing and we hung on,
admiring the vistas of being away
while the shadows died down from the flames of day
and we coasted around a long headland of sky
and into night's port while, out in the bay
tomorrow called out like a ringing buoy.

The Reference Library
(to open the sixth-form library at Ysgol Gyfun Rhydfelen)

Elsewhere a leather-bound volume holds the sum
of what a distant century knew
of cosmology and Christendom,
of how to cook with feverfew;

how to make silk; how Latin spread
like roads across a kingdom which then fell
to rhetoric and laws and lead
but let prophetic fishes tell

their older stories, ones of mortal sin,
how men of rock were spawned from tors
with tongues of granite, breathing whin
which stopped the logical conquerors.

How comprehensive! Look around you now:
concordances are a thumbnail wide,
a wafer-thin thesaurus shows you how
new languages are regicides;

there are directories of heads of state,
files of disease with their listed cures,
transport technologies to contemplate,
anatomies of the urban poor . . .

But compared to you, an encyclopaedia
is thin provision. Throw the big tomes out,
and the almanacs with their logorrhoea.
Read first the lexicons of your own doubt,

for in your spines and not in those of books,
lies the way to live well, the best library;
for the erudition of your open looks
shall turn old words to new theologies.

Pentecost

The Lord wants me to go to Florida.
I shall cross the border with the mercury thieves,
as foretold in the faxes and prophecies,
and the checkpoint angel of Estonia
will have alerted the uniformed birds
to act unnatural and distract the guards

so I pass unhindered. My glossolalia
shall be my passport – I shall taste the tang
of travel on the atlas of my tongue –
salt Poland, sour Denmark and sweet Vienna
and all men in the Spirit shall understand
that, in His wisdom, the Lord has sent

a slip of a girl to save great Florida.
I shall tear through Europe like a standing flame,

not pausing for long, except to rename
the occasional city; in Sofia
thousands converted and hundreds slain
in the Holy Spirit along the Seine.

My life is your chronicle; O Florida
revived, look forward to your past,
and prepare your perpetual Pentecost
of golf course and freeway, shopping mall and car
so the fires that are burning in the orange groves
turn light into sweetness and the huddled graves

are the hives of the future – an America
spelt plainly, translated in the Everglades
where palm fruit hang like hand grenades
ready to rip whole treatises of air.
Then the S in the tail of the crocodile
will make perfect sense to the bibliophile

who will study this land, his second Torah.
All this was revealed. Now I wait for the Lord
to move heaven and earth to send me abroad
and fulfil His bold promise to Florida.
As I stay put, He shifts His continent:
Atlantic closes, the sheet of time is rent.

Good Dog!

All pets are part of one animal.
They look out at us from domestic eyes
hoping for food and a little love.
People who believe in reincarnation
feel the concern of departed relatives
shine from the heart of new-born pups,
so confide in them, spoil them.
A well-placed 'Om' in a mongrel's ear
can save the soul of a dying dog.

Ours is theologian. He knows
that sticks in life are more reliable than cats
and that balls are better. Everything thrown
is instantly precious, well worth running for.
The river he loves and tends to wear
it often. A Baptist, he immerses himself
with total abandon so his otter soul
is renewed in the feeder with the bags of crisps
and ribbons of algae.
He wears the medal of himself with joy.

Something there is about a dog
draws conversation from frosty men
and available women. Trick for lonely boys and girls:
Get a dog. Walk him. For be it ugly or pure-bred,
a dog on a lead says: 'Here is a love
that makes its bargain with bad habits and smells,
the brute in a person, can accommodate needs
far other than its own, allows for beastliness.'

Some nights our lodger gets his favourite ball,
runs into the river and tramples the moon.

Mudrooroo

Australian Aboriginal – 1939-

Born in Western Australia in 1938, Mudrooroo Nyoongah is best known as a novelist. He won fame with his first novel, *Wildcat Falling*, published under his European name, Colin Johnson; his best novel is undoubtedly *Doctor Wooredy's Prescription for Enduring the Ending of the World*. He has published several volumes of verse, including *The Garden of Gethsemane* (Hyland House, 1991) and *Pacific Highway Boo-Blooz* (University of Queensland Press, 1996).

A Righteous Day

A lifetime of inventions sticky-taping a zipper into
A ballpoint pen filled with transistorised tunes
Protecting my wrists from the slashes of insecurities.
Today, I shall hold my head higher than
The kites are flying, swooping down on this
Today, I shall keep my violence passive in anger,
My voice shall be a steel spring coiled.
Today, I shall cut a smile into the provocation of insults.
Today, I shall walk tall with the leaders who walk on
Stilts and stumble as they greet me with cries of goodwill.
Today, I shall stand sober and high under the railway bridge
Echoing and resounding with the slap-slap of straight razors
Stropping on the skin of a year mourning bleeding.
Today, I shall let my fist be clenched in songs;
Today, I shall speech-give the essence of my truth;
Today, I shall be free of harassment and let my steps
Lead me away from the red and black along the golden path
Of the honeyed sunshining of my dreams.
Today, I shall find a will to be responsive to our needs.
For today, this day is our day and don't forget it!
'My bloody oath I won't, mate!'

(Sydney, 26 January 1988)

The Ultimate Demonstration

A very important day,
Black and white together:
beautiful!

Your hands meet in so many faces,
Black and white the ultimate funeral
Waking the injustices of the past
Into a future linking us as one nation.

If all were here, not there,
Together in the survival of 200 years
Messaging the concern for the land.

Hey, Australia, 200 years of birthing a nation
Far older than your wiles.
200 years is less than a piece of shit,
Without curing the ills of division,
Without meeting the outstretching hand
Of those who never landed at the command from a king.

Let us pray: the land is boss;
Let us pray: the land is victorious;
Let us pray: the land needs no birthdays.
Too old to remember the day it was born,
Too old to forget the people it birthed.

Let you understand, our ancientness;
Let you understand, the simple justice of being
Here as the thousands of years move past
In our languages, in our ceremonies, in our celebrations:
Black and white together in a fruitful thankfulness
For our greatness rising and setting forth our unity

(26 January 1988)

Tracks

Muddy tracks, rain marks end-traces
In runnels, in tunnels, in seethings
Flowing, drifting, edging, turning, oozing
Into the ocean, dark felt-lined by lacy
Identifications in the night of torch-flickering
Faint tracks, lithe tracks, lines of consonants,
Torch-flickering, the pages flickering,
Teething a hard line eliminating.
The meandering track grows trees
And grass and weeds and legs grappling
Burrs and times out of time,
As the track, snaking, twisting,
Moving away into a past of hand writing
Circling about a history of geology
Stratified into emotions paste-like,
Settling down into silt, oozing,
Seething, spreading liquidification;
Settling down, the rain marks end-traces,
As the road cuts straight towards once goals,
Now gone, as that road removes
The runnels, the tunnels in tired dreams
Tarred and cemented into the solid sediments
Of hard rock dissolving into soft sea.

Who?

Who knocked at my walls,
Tapped at my door,
Broke my loneliness?

Who came hesitantly,
Conscious of a need to evade
Any hidden intrusions?

Who concealed himself from the opening door,
The spilling of life,
The dappled darkness without
Breathing sighs of a broken love?

Who roamed absurdly around the walls,
Trying the windows, the cracks, the locks
In a sudden confidence of suspicion
At the slight rustling in the undergrowth
Signalling other strangers with other intentions?

Who came and went without entering;
Who came risking all for a single glance,
Then left as the gale dissipated the clouds
And moon light flooded broadly through the senses
To dissipate any issues which might be forced?

Quietness

The felt middle current of quietness;
The constant bass drone of the ocean;
The shrillness of cicadas calling lost lovers
From the harsh croaking of frogs entwining
With the patter of yet more rain,
Suddenly emerging into my whisper
As I sit, a scratch of a pen on a page:
Whispered written words
Not needing the return of answers.
I feel my being entire and complete,
Part of the quietness, the drone,
The shrillness, the croaking and the patter.
Now, not seeking to ask questions,
Just being, here-and-now, while a vehicle
Erupts in anger at skimming over, but never with.

Hide and Seek

Hidden in hidden rooms,
Afraid to face
A glimmer of truth,
Wives and kids
Hardly speaking a word,
Except to demand.
Speak, reply, mumble.
Once men were mythologies;
Once spears were clutched;
Once our words ran together,
In complex sentences of intent;
Now we have become monosyllables,
Lonely in straight streets,
As long as the sentences
We once formed
From our initiation marks,
Cut deeply into our living flesh,
By masters of our languages.

City Suburban Lines

Their roads are straight;
Their streets are straight;
Their fences are straight;
Straight are the bricks
Of their walls,
As straight as the lines
Of their vehicle-minds,
Rushing in straight thoughts
To straight feelings.

Unholy is their straightness;
Their religion is straight,
Bound between straight

Lines in a book whose prose
Has been straightened,
And made to move along
The straightness of their lives.

Straight are the pictures on their walls;
Straight, ensquaring lines unfeelingly straight
With moods straight from the strayed lines
Of tended gardens straight with the stems
Of flowers modified into straightness.

Straight is the world they have fashioned;
Straight are the walls of their imprisoning cells;
Straight are the lives we are forced to endure:
Born between straight lines;
Dying between straight lines;
Laid to rest between straight lines,
Buried in rows as straight as supermarket goods:
Our heaven will be straight lines;
Our hell will be all curved lines,
Unable to fit the straightness of our souls.

Dennis O'Driscoll

Irish – 1954-

Born in County Tipperary, Dennis O'Driscoll is considered one of the most outstanding of the younger generation of Irish poets. He has published four volumes of verse: *Kist* (Dolmen Press,1982), *Hidden Extras* (Anvil, 1987), *Long Story Short* (Anvil, 1993), *Quality Time* (Anvil, 1997).

In Office

We are marching for work:
people fresh from dream bedrooms,
people whose flesh begins to slip
like old linoleum loosening on a floor,
people with head colds and lovebites,
girls startlingly immaculate,
pores probed with cleanser,
ribboned hair still wet;
people submitting their tastes and talents
to the demands of office,
the uniform grind of files.

We forego identity and drive
for the security of such places,
a foyer guard by the spotlit tapestry;
soft furnishings; a constant heat;
gossip with the copier's undulations;
crushes on new recruits; booze-ups
after back-pay from disputes . . .
We are wasting our lives
earning a living, underwriting new life,
grateful at a time of unemployment
to have jobs, hating what we do.

Work is the nightmare from which we yearn to wake,
the slow hours between tea-breaks
vetting claims, scrutinising VDUs.
We are the people at the other end
of telephone extensions when you ring,
the ones who put a good face on the firm,
responding to enquiries, parrying complaints,
the ones without the luck to have inherited
long-laned retreats, fixed-income bonds,
who yield to lunchtime temptations,
buy clothes and gadgets, keep retail spending high.

We age in the mirrors of office lavatories
watch seeds of rain broadcast their flecks
along the screen of tinted glass, a pane
that stands between us and the freedom
which we struggle towards
and will resign ourselves to
when the clock comes round.

Fruit Salad

I   PEACH

There's not much point in trying
to cultivate a sultry peach of words.
Just pass me one to stroke, to eat,
or paint it from a glowing palette;
colours dart from apricot to apple,
flames licking velvet hide.
Hold its downy, yielding roundness,
fondle its lightly clothed contours,
taste its golden mean, its sweetness,
before it starts to shrink and shrivel,
starts to wrinkle like a passion fruit.

II STRAWBERRY

Strawberries with whipped cream,
a sunset ripple on your plate...
A cordate locket, a precious stone;
cut one and expose the marbled core.
The wholesome rubicundity of outdoors,
not the hothouse plastic of tomatoes;
compact, meaty, flecked with seeds,
the bracts a garnish (parsley on beef,
verdant ferns in a bouquet of roses).
A July day provides the ideal accompaniment
lazy as the cream dripping from the whisk.

III PEAR

Most easily hurt of fruits,
bruising under a matt coat of skin,
smooth as bath soap inside;
halved, a perfectly stringed lute.
It hangs in a shaft of autumn light
timeless as a bronze cathedral bell
or disturbs the peace and drops
– a hand grenade, pin still intact,
a toppling shell of glycerine.
We take refuge from our troubles in its syrup
wasps burrowing through heady pulp.

IV APPLE

All apples lead back to that first temptation
trees behind the thatched farmhouse,
forbidden fruit, a warts-and-all beauty,
pupating in pink silk blossom
then fired and glazed in summer,
brushed by a red admiral's wings,

wine-dipped like nectarines or green
as nettles stinging with tart knowledge.
Bite the way back to a primal silence,
your rhythmic crunch shutting out
the world, digesting its hard truths.

V   FRUIT SHOP

Orange skins baked to a crust
(fluffy whiteness underneath);
raspberries like bleeding gums;
melons whose haunches
are tested for ripeness...
I buy bananas racked like chops
and apricots, one blemished
with a spot (which I'll slice off,
cheddar flesh wholesome again).
I pinch a bulbous, plum-sized grape.
Lemons tumble from an opened crate.

Operation

I removed slates
tight as muscle fibre,
opened a flap of skull.
There was a fungal whiff,
sprinklings of wood
like bone dust
on the vascular wires.

Fresh views had not
been aired in this
cramped space for years,
a fine grey matter smeared

the brittle beams,
dotted lines left
signs of worms.

No wonder the roof
had sagged abstractedly:
the house was brain-dead
though its heart
continued to beat
regularly as feet
clambering up the stairs.

Looking Forward

We have already advanced
to the stage where we can
convene seminars on cost/yield ratio
and child sexual abuse.
We have reached the point
where genetic engineering can create
a tender, tasty, waste-free sow,
a rindless cut above the rest.
It certainly is not the experts' fault
if minds, like power supplies, break down
under the strain of our pace of life
or if bodies are stifled by the human crush
– tears like oil welling from rock –
or if hunger sears as soils erode:
remember the humblest shanty town
is still the corrugated product
of great skill and ingenuity.
Desert missile tests or rocket launches
may, on rare occasions, prove disastrous;
but we are capable of learning from mistakes
and will get things right the next time.
The alienated are just slow developers,
suffering the growing pains of evolution.
Out of the dung heap of chemical spills,
a thornless mutant rose will sprout,
its scent as fragrant as a new deodorant spray.

Case Studies

I

It is easier to prove the existence
of leukaemia than of God

and so I pan for God
in the gold marrow of bald children

who trust in Him with passive smiles
above their Donald Duck pyjama tops,

faces magnified to corpuscles of dots
in yellowing newspaper photographs.

II

Add to the accidents
read about or known

and multiply by all the victims
named in phone-calls to expectant parents

the crushing death of this young woman
whose body was reduced to slush

as the bus she ran for registered
her minute impact with its wheels.

III

Dawn blinks into existence
like an intravenous drip.

The water trolley rattles,
constellations of beads

clouded in condensation.
Beside one bed, a draught of urine:

red vintage wine
decanted for analysis.

IV

Her chances dim under theatre lights
as she hangs on to life

by a slim surgical thread.
Past childhood rashes, teenage acne,

illnesses of old age strike home,
planted – like bulbs of ova – before birth.

A riddling which, her world
turned upside down, death solves.

Elegies

I

sapling
that was rooted
at his birth

is ready to yield
a coffin now:
its rings

like ripples spread
to count
his submerged years

II

we are digging
on this spring day
burying an exhausted gardener

his stiffly-folded
cigarette-stained fingers
brown as clay

the weeping cherry
he planted
beginning to bud

III

a snowdrop host
our only solid food
melts in the mouth

we are drunk
on altar wine
a rare blood group

seeking strength to face
the gathering crowds
of dead

IV

he is stored
in the gold bullion
of an oak coffin

overhead the earth's scars heal
flowers are dyeing fields
a road worker is in full song

and only we can tell
that sunlight casts
one shadow less

Premonitions

I

Sometimes I stand
in a draught of death:
it wafts through my body

as a premonition
and I shudder like a fridge,
catching its cold.

II

The birth wards swell,
slippery with life,
and every vacancy is filled

so that our absence
will not be noticed
in the changing crowd.

III

This breeze will blow
its loneliness through trees
long after we are shrouded.

Your mourning eyes,
black-rimmed as memorial cards,
will find a deeper sleep.

IV

Each death proves
death still lives,
when lives regular

as breathing stop;
stocking flags triumphant
on the leg-bones' staff.

What She Does Not Know Is

That she is a widow
That these are the last untinged memories of her life.
That he is slumped in his seat at a lay-by.
That a policeman is trying to revive him.
That the knife and fork she has set are merely decorative.
That the liver beside the pan will be left to rot.
That he has lost his appetite.
That the house she is tidying is for sale.
That the holiday photograph will be used for his memorial card.
That his sunburned body will not be subjected to direct light again.
That she will spend all night brewing tears.
That is not his car she will soon hear slowing down outside.

Janos Pilinszky

Hungarian – 1921-1981

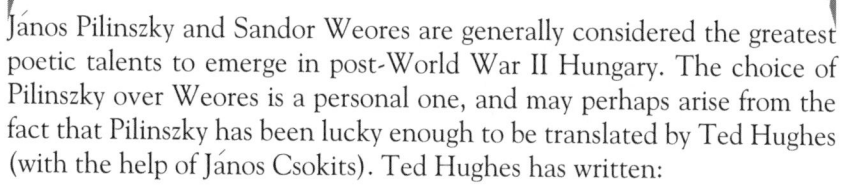

János Pilinszky and Sandor Weores are generally considered the greatest poetic talents to emerge in post-World War II Hungary. The choice of Pilinszky over Weores is a personal one, and may perhaps arise from the fact that Pilinszky has been lucky enough to be translated by Ted Hughes (with the help of János Csokits). Ted Hughes has written:

> The quality of [Pilinszky's] actual style is an essence, from the heart of his vision. It is direct, simple, even 'impoverished', but all Hungarians agree that it is a marvel of luminosity, unerring balance, sinuous music and intensity – a metal resembling nothing else. Through translation we can only try to imagine that...

Like several other poets in this collection, Pilinszky's vision was forever altered by his experiences during the Second World War. Conscripted into the army (Hungary had been absorbed into the empire of the Third Reich) he was eventually taken prisoner and spent the last year of the war in prison camps in Austria and Germany.

> After this experience there emerges, at the heart of his poems, a strange creature, 'a gasping, limbless trunk', savaged by primal hungers, among the odds and ends of a destroyed culture, waiting to be shot, or beaten to death, or just thrown on a refuse heap...
>
> (Ted Hughes)

Another important influence was religion: like most Hungarians, Pilinszky was brought up a Catholic.

Fable

Once upon a time
there was a lonely wolf
lonelier than the angels.

He happened to come to a village.
He fell in love with the first house he saw.

Already he loved its walls
the caresses of its bricklayers.
But the window stopped him.

In the room sat people.
Apart from God nobody ever
found them so beautiful
as this child-like beast.

So at night he went into the house.
He stopped in the middle of the room
and never moved from there any more.

He stood all through the night, with wide eyes
and on into the morning when he was beaten to death.

Fish in the Net

We are tossing in a net of stars.
Fish hauled up to the beach,
gasping in nothingness,
mouths snapping dry void.
Whispering, the lost element
calls us in vain.
Choking among edged stones
and pebbles we must
live and die in a heap.
Our hearts convulse.
Our writhings maim
and suffocate our brother.
Our cries conflict but

not even an echo answers.
We have no reason
to fight and kill
but we must.
So we atone but our atonement
does not suffice.
No suffering
can redeem our hells.
We are tossing in a starry net
and at midnight
maybe we shall lie on the table
of a mighty fisherman.

The French Prisoner

If only I could forget that Frenchman.
I saw him, a little before dawn, creeping past our hut
into the dense growth of the back garden
so that he almost merged into the ground.
As I watched he looked back, he peered all round –
at last he had found a safe hideout.
Now his plunder can be all his!
Whatever happens, he'll go no further.

And already he is eating, biting into the turnip
which he must have smuggled out under his rags.
He was gulping raw cattle-turnip!
Yet he had hardly swallowed one mouthful
before it vomited back up.
Then the sweet pulp in his mouth mingled
with joy and revulsion the same
as the happy and unhappy are coupled
in their bodies' ravenous ecstasy.

Only to forget that body, those convulsed shoulder blades,
the hands shrunk to bone,
the bare palm that crammed at his mouth, and clung there
so that it ate, too.
And the shame, desperate, furious,
of the organs savaging each other,
forced to tear from each other
their last shreds of kinship.

The way his clumsy feet had been left out
of the gibbering, bestial elation –
and splayed there, squashed beneath
the torture and rapture of his body.
And his glance – if only I could forget that!
Though he was choking, he kept on
forcing more down his gullet – no matter what –
only to eat – anything – this – that – even himself!

Why go on. Guards came for him.
He had escaped from the nearby prison camp.
And just as I did then, in that garden,
I am strolling here, among garden shadows, at home.
I look into my notes and quote:
'If only I could forget that Frenchman.....'
And from my ears, from my eyes, my mouth
the scorching memory roars at me:

'I am hungry!' And suddenly I feel
the everlasting hunger
that poor creature has long since forgotten
and which no earthly nourishment can lessen.
He lives on me. And more and more hungrily!
And I am less and less sufficient for him.
And now he, who would have eaten anything,
is yelling for my heart.

Passion of Ravensbrück

He steps out from the others.
He stands in the square silence.
The prison garb, the convict's
skull
blink like a projection.

He is horribly alone.
His pores are visible.
Everything about him is so gigantic,
everything is so tiny.

And this is all.
                The rest –
the rest was simply
that he forgot to cry out
before he collapsed.

The Desert of Love

A bridge, and a hot concrete road –
the day is emptying its pockets,
laying out, one by one, all its possessions.
You are quite alone in the catatonic twilight.

A landscape like the bed of a wrinkled pit,
with glowing scars, a darkness which dazzles.
Dusk thickens. I stand numb with brightness
blinded by the sun. This summer will not leave me,

Summer. And the flashing heat.
The chickens stand, like burning cherubs,
in the boarded-up, splintered cages.
I know their wings do not even tremble.

Do you still remember? First there was the wind.
And then the earth. Then the cage.
Flames, dung. And now and again
a few wing-flutters, a few empty reflexes.

And thirst. I asked for water.
Even today I hear that feverish gulping,
and helplessly, like a stone, bear
and quench the mirages.

Years are passing. And years. And hope
is like a tin-cup toppled into the straw.

Revelations VIII.7

and God sees the burning heaven
and against it birds flying
and he sees sinking deeper and deeper
 those too weak to cross the disc of fire

and from end to end
In a redness of copper broken to fragments
where a man hoeing will never be found again
he sees the earth and once again the earth

the desert and the chaos
and a horse and cart searching to wade out
but God sees there is no way
or road or hope to break from this vision!

Gradually

As the nothingness soothes over
the ditches of the death-struggle,
as the fields after a blizzard
calm down and find their way home again,
somehow, in just such a gradual way,
growing plain and simple, unfolds
the dialogue of God and man,
destruction and birth.

Tadeusz Różewicz

Polish – 1921-

Poland's losses in the Second World War were greater even than Russia's, with almost 25% of the population dying. Hence any poet coming to maturity in those terrible years would be indelibly marked by the experience and much of Różewicz's poetry is, in his words, "poetry for the horror-stricken. For those abandoned to butchery. For survivors." Like the Hungarian poet Pilinszky, born in the same year, Różewicz has forged a poetic diction that is simple and direct, but also charged with ambiguity. His poetry has been translated into English by Adam Czerniawski.

Mars

A room

a family
of five or six

someone's reading a book
someone's looking at photographs
someone remembers the war
someone's falling asleep someone leaves
someone 's dying in the silence
someone's drinking water
someone's breaking bread
Tommy writes the letter A
and draws a knight with a blue spur
someone's getting ready to go to the moon
someone's brought a rose a bird a fish
it's snowing
a bell tolls

Mars appears
his sword
fills the room
with fire

The Survivor

I am twenty-four
led to slaughter
I survived.

The following are empty synonyms:
man and beast
love and hate
friend and foe
darkness and light.

The way of killing men and beasts is the same
I've seen it:
truckfuls of chopped-up men
who will not be saved.

Ideas are mere words:
virtue and crime
truth and lies
beauty and ugliness
courage and cowardice.

Virtue and crime weigh the same
I've seen it:
in a man who was both
criminal and virtuous.

I seek a teacher and a master
may he restore my sight hearing and speech
may he again name objects and ideas
may he separate darkness from light.

I am twenty-four
led to slaughter
I survived.

Abattoirs

Pink quartered ideals
hang in abattoirs

Shops are selling
clowns'
motley death-masks

stripped off the faces
of us who live
who have survived
staring
into the eye-socket of war.

Posthumous Rehabilitation

The dead have remembered
our indifference
The dead have remembered
our silence
The dead have remembered
our words

The dead see our snouts
laughing from ear to ear
The dead see
our bodies rubbing against each other
The dead hear
clucking tongues

The dead read our books
listen to our speeches
delivered so long ago

The dead scrutinize our lectures
join in previously terminated
discussions
The dead see our hands
poised for applause

The dead see stadiums
ensembles and choirs declaiming rhythmically

all the living are guilty

little children
who offered bouquets of flowers
are guilty
lovers are guilty
guilty are poets

guilty are those who ran away
and those that stayed
those who were saying yes
those who said no
and those who said nothing

the dead are taking stock of the living
the dead will not rehabilitate us

A Tree

Happy were
the poets of old
the world like a tree
they like a child

What shall I hang
upon the branch of a tree
which has suffered
a rain of steel

Happy were
the poets of old
around the tree
they danced like a child

What shall I hang
upon the branch of a tree
which is burnt
and never will sing

Happy were
the poets of old
beneath the oak
they sang like a child

But our tree
creaked in the night
with the weight
of a corpse despised

Massacre of the Boys

The children cried 'Mummy!
But I have been good!
It's dark in here! Dark!'

See them They are going to the bottom
See the small feet
they went to the bottom Do you see
that print
of a small foot here and there

pockets bulging,
with string and stones
and little horses made of wire

A great closed plain
like a figure of geometry
and a tree of black smoke
a vertical
dead tree
with no star in its crown.

The Museum, Auschwitz, 1948

Pigtail

When all the women in the transport
had their heads shaved
four workmen with brooms made of birch twigs
swept up
and gathered up the hair

Behind clean glass
the stiff hair lies
of those suffocated in gas chambers
there are pins and side combs
in this hair

The hair is not shot through with light
is not parted by the breeze
is not touched by any hand
or rain or lips

In huge chests
clouds of dry hair
of those suffocated
and a faded plait
a pigtail with a ribbon
pulled at school
by naughty boys.

The Museum, Auschwitz, 1948

Grass

I grow
in the bondings of walls
where they are
joined
there where they meet
there where they are vaulted

there I penetrate
a blind seed
scattered by the wind

patiently I spread
in the cracks of silence
I wait for the walls to fall
and return to earth

then I will cover
names and faces

What Luck

What luck I can pick
berries in the wood
I thought
there is no wood no berries.

What luck I can lie
in the shade of a tree
I thought trees
no longer give shade.

What luck I am with you
my heart beats so
I thought man
has no heart.

Re-education

the poet speaks
the same language to

a child
a provocateur
a priest
a politician
a policeman

the child smiles
the provocateur feels ridiculed
the politician slighted
the priest threatened
the policeman buttons up his coat

the embarrassed poet
asks forgiveness
and repeats
his mistake

Completion

This side
is turned towards others
and though it is worn
changeable counterfeit
it gives an idea
of my shape

the other side
which no one knows
which will never see
the light of day
which unto death
and after death will not be touched by others

that other side
known only to me
remains hidden
but influences the side which is
revealed
and through it communicates with other people

Who
surprised
amused
appalled

exclaim

fancy his being like that
it's not at all like him
this must be someone else

in the familiar portrait
a new ambiguous feature has appeared
startling
and completing

Vittorio Sereni

Italian – 1913-1983

Perhaps the finest Italian poet of his generation, Vittorio Sereni served in the Italian Army during the Second World War and was captured when the Allies invaded Sicily. Sereni was never a fascist, and it is not difficult to detect in his verse a feeling of guilt that he was not able to join the anti-fascist partisans, particularly once Mussolini had fallen and the Germans had occupied Northern Italy. His *Selected Poems* appeared in English in 1990, translated by Marcus Perryman and Peter Robinson (Anvil).

First Fear

Every corner or alley, every
        moment's good
for the killer who's been stalking me
night and day for years.
Shoot me, shoot me – I tell him
offering myself to his aim
in the front, the side, the back –
let's get it over with, do me in.
And saying it I realize
I'm talking to myself alone.
        But
it's no use, it's no use. On my own
I cannot bring myself to justice.

Second Fear

There's nothing terrifying
about the voice that beckons me
and no one else
from the street below my home
at some hour of night:
it's a wind's brief wakening,
a fleeting shower.
In speaking my name it doesn't list
my misdeeds, rebuke me for my past.
With tenderness (Vittorio,
Vittorio) it disarms me, is arming
me myself against me.

A Dream

I was crossing the bridge
over a river that could have been the Magra
where I go for the summer, or even the Tresa,
in my part of the country between Germignaga and Luino.
A leaden body without face blocked my way.
'Papers,' he ordered. 'What papers,' I answered.
'Out with them,' he insisted, firm,
on seeing me look aghast. I made to appease him
'I've prospects, a place awaiting me,
certain memories, friends still alive,
a few dead honourably buried.'
'Fairy tales,' – he said – 'you can't pass
without a programme.' And sneering he weighed
the few papers, my worldly goods.
I wanted one last try. 'I'll pay
on my way back if you'll let me
pass, if you'll let me work.'
We would never see eye to eye: 'Have you made'
– he was snarling – 'your ideological choice?'
Grappling we struggled on the bridge's parapet
in utter solitude. The fight
still goes on, to my dishonour.
I don't know
who'll end up in the river.

Six in the Morning

Death breaks the seal, just so, of everything.
And in fact, I came back,
the door wasn't properly shut
the panel barely ajar.
And in fact I'd been dead a short while,
done for in not many hours.
But what I saw, plainly,

the dead don't see:
visited by my recent death, the house
only barely disturbed
still warm with me who no longer existed,
the bar snapped,
purposeless the bolt
and a great and peopled atmosphere
about me, little in death,
one after another the avenues
of Milan awakened in all that wind.

Those Children Playing

will one day forgive
if we soon get out of the way.
They'll forgive. One day.
But the time's twistedness,
life's course deviated down false tracks,
the haemorrhage of days
from the pass of corrupted awareness:
this, no, they won't forgive.
You don't forgive a woman for deceitful love,
the smiling land of water and leaves
that's torn apart revealing
putrefied roots, black slime.
'In love there are no sins',
raged a poet in his final years,
'there are only sins against love.'
And these, no, they will not forgive.

Madrigal to Nefertiti

Where will it be, with whom the smile
which seems if it touches me
to know all about me,
past, future, but is oblivious of the present
should I attempt to tell her what waters
for me it becomes between palms and dunes
and emerald shores
– and she turns it back onto a yesterday
of enchantments, remnants, smoke
or postpones it until a tomorrow
which will not belong to me
and of something quite other if I speak to her, speaks?

Those Thoughts of Yours of Calamity

and catastrophe
in the house where you have
come to live, already
occupied
by the idea of having come
here to die
– and these who smile at you, friends,
surely this time
you're dying, they know it, and that's why
they're smiling.

From Holland
Amsterdam

Chance led me there between
nine and ten one Sunday morning,
turning at a bridge, one of many, to the right
along a canal half iced over. And not
this is the house, but merely
– seen a thousand times before –
'Anne Frank's house', on the simple plaque.

Later my companion said:
Anne Frank's shouldn't be, it isn't
a privileged memory. There were many
were broken simply out of hunger
without the time to write.
She, it's true, did write it.
But at every turn, at every bridge, along every canal
I continued to search for her, no longer finding her,
finding her perpetually.
That's why it's one and unfathomable Amsterdam
in its three or four varying elements
which it blends in many recurring wholes,
its three or four rotten or unripe colours
which its space perpetuates far as it stretches,
spirit that irradiates steadfast and clear
on thousands of other faces, everywhere
seed and bud of Anne Frank.
That's why Amsterdam's vertiginous on its canals.

Xuan Quynh
Vietnamese – 1942-1988

Most modern Vietnamese poetry draws its subject matter from the turbulent and tragic war years: the fight to cast off the colonial power, France, in the post-World War II years, the struggle between North and South Vietnam and the conflict with the USA. In contrast, much of Xuan Quynh's writing turns aside from the struggle and deals with personal themes. Trained as a dancer, she published several books of verse. She and her husband, another Vietnamese poet, were killed in a car crash in 1988.

Readers interested in becoming acquainted with other Vietnamese poets of the period should seek out the anthology *Mountain River: Vietnamese poetry from the wars, 1948-1993* ed. Kevin Bowen, Nguyen Ba Chung and Bruce Weigl (Amherst: University of Massachusetts Press, 1998.)

Worried Over the Days Past

Many went to see their lovers off,
Their trucks disappeared into the border region.
My love too was a soldier,
But I was not there when he left.

Those days, you hadn't reached me yet!
Sixteen years old, the pages of your diary full;
You wrote about the streets, the young lovers.
Was there anything there you wrote of me?

An old story – you'd already forgotten.
You had no complaints, only a little sadness.
I wish I could have been those blades of grass
Swaying along the road as you left.

I wish I could have been a forest with grand canopies,
Or a spring by the scorching paths to cool you.
I wish I could have been a lullaby when you slept,
Singing our mother's old songs

When the forest fever yellowed your eyes and blackened your skin,
I would be your comrade to bring you a cup of cool water.
I would be the grain of dust along the road you walked,
A roof to cover you from the rain,
A rice satchel hung over your shoulder when you were hungry,
A flame lighting the darkness in the forest ahead.
My love for you is beyond telling:
Like the blue sky – the blue unfathomable sky.
Even now when I have you by my side
And we share our common worries, dreams, and joys,
I still worry about those days,
Days when you hadn't reached me yet.

(Nguyen Ba Chung and Kevin Bowen)

The Co May Flower

The sands deserted, river high, trees in a daze.
The heavens stir the season's change.
Behind the canopy, who calls my name?
I return on the old road, bending into autumn.

White clouds float away on the wind,
The heart is like the emerald sky at creation.
Let's leave that bitterness and hardship to seasons past,
Let those lines of poetry float away on the wind.

Everywhere the co may flowers are in bloom.
Careless, I let the grasses prick my shirt.
Words of love run like wisps of smoke.
Who can tell the heart's changes?

(Nguyen Ba Chung and Kevin Bowen)

Wave

Fierce and gentle,
Loud and silent,
The river doesn't understand itself.
The wave doesn't find itself, until it reaches the sea.

Oh the wave passes,
And the waves to come will be the same.
Hunger for love
Is strong in the heart.

Standing before the waves,
I think of you and me.
I think of the great sea
And I wonder where the waves come from.

The waves must come from the wind.
And I wonder where the wind comes from,
And I wonder
When will we love each other again?

The waves deep in the sea
And the waves on the sea's surface
Long for the shore of the sea.
Day and night the waves cannot sleep
As I cannot sleep, even in dreams,
Because of my longing for you.

When I go to the North,
Or to the South,
When I go anywhere, I think of you,
My only direction.

Out in that great sea
Thousands of waves are pushing,
Which one never reaches the shore
Even miles and miles from home?

Life is so long;
Years and months go by.
Like the sea, life is endless.
Clouds fly to the distant horizon.

How can I become
Like the hundreds of thousands of small waves
In the great sea of love
And lap forever against your shore?

                (Nguyen Quang Thieu, Nguyen Ba Chung, and Bruce Weigl)

Part 2: Variations on Traditional Stories

As we have seen, poets as different as Sujata Bhatt and Ivan Lalić often draw on the great myths, legends and folk stories of the world for their subject matter. In this section we look at some other poets who provide new slants on traditional stories.

Orpheus Opens His Morning Mail
Donald Justice

Bills. Bills. From the mapmakers of hell, the repairers of fractured lutes, the bribed judges of musical contests, etc.

A note addressed to my wife, marked: *Please Forward.*

A group photograph, signed: *Your Admirers.* In their faces a certain sameness, as if 'i' might, after all, be raised to some modest power; likewise in their costumes, at once transparent and identical, like those of young ladies at some debauched seminary. Already – such is my vice – I imagine the rooms into which they must once have locked themselves to read my work: those barren cells, beds ostentatiously unmade; the single pinched chrysanthemum, memorializing in a corner some withered event; the mullioned panes, high up, through which may be spied, far off, the shorn hedge behind which a pimply tomorrow crouches, exposing himself. O lassitudes!

Finally, an invitation to attend certain rites to be celebrated, come equinox, on the river bank. I am to be guest of honour. As always, I rehearse the scene in advance: the dark, the hired guards, tipsy as usual, sonorously snoring; a rustling, suddenly, among the reeds; the fitful illumination of ankles, whitely flashing ... Afterwards, I shall probably be asked to recite my poems. But O my visions, my vertigoes! Have I imagined it only, the perverse gentility of their shrieks?

Cinderella
Gwen Strauss

My step-sisters are willing
to cut off their toes for him.

What would I do for those days
when I played alone
in the hazel tree over my mother's grave?

I would go backwards if I could
and stay in that moment when the doves
fluttered down with the golden gown.

But everything has changed.
I trace his form in the ashes,
and then sweep it away before they see.

He's been on parade with that shoe.
All Prince, with heralds and entourage,
they come trumpeting through the village.

If he found me, would he recognize me,
my face, after mistaking their feet for mine?
I want to crawl away

into my pigeon house, my pear tree.
The world is too large, bright like a ballroom
and then suddenly dark.

Mother, no one prepared me for this –
for the soft heat of a man's neck when he dances
or the thickness of his arms.

Cinders
Sue Stewart

Like the horses I revert to type at midnight,
combing mousey hair. This too was written
in his kiss, my slipper's made-to-measure.

Servants' eyes are discreet but not their whispers;
I'm too easy with them, then sharp when the smell
of polish threatens to take me back. Alone,
I stroke the grain of my chair's buffed arm,
cup its lion's paw in mine as my husband breezes in,
rakish as he feels it his duty to be. He brings news
of our estate like a fresh bouquet – fresh as his collar,
where a vermilion mouth blooms, or as my Two Uglies,
trimmed and pinked.

Newly enslaved, I look for ways to explain myself –
the loneliness of the rich, my absent spouse –
and let sisterhood cloud my thoughts
as the gypsophila this vase, or the hollyhocks the sky,
which I scarcely dare approach.

The Waiting Wolf
Gwen Strauss

First, I saw her feet –
beneath a red pointed cloak
head bent forward
parting the woods,
one foot placed straight
in front of the other.

Then, came her scent.
I was meant to stalk her
smooth, not a twig snaps.
It is the only way I know;
I showed her flowers –

white dead-nettle, nightshade,
devil's bit, wood anemone.

I might not have gone further,
but then nothing ever remains
innocent in the woods.

When she told me about Grandmother,
I sickened. She placed herself on my path,
practically spilling her basket of breads and jams.

Waiting in this old lady's ruffled bed,
I am all calculation. I have gone this far –
dressed in Grandmother's lace panties,
flannel nightgown and cap,
puffs of breath beneath the sheet
lift and fall. I can see my heart tick.
Slightly. Slightly.

These are small lies for a wolf,
but strangely heavy in my belly like stones.
I will forget them as soon as I have her,
still, at this moment I do not like myself.

When she crawls into Grandma's bed,
will she pull me close, thinking:
This is my grandmother whom I love?

She will have the youngest skin
I have ever touched, her fingers unfurling
like fiddle heads in spring.

My matted fur will smell to her of forest
moss at night. She'll wonder about my ears,
large, pointed, soft as felt,
my eyes red as her cloak,
my leather nose on her belly.

But perhaps she has known who I am since the first,
since we took the other path
through the woods.

Inside Wolf
Sue Stewart

I lose a shoe on the way in, as sign – my one
mistake – then teeter on his tongue's root
and dive into cramped air, counting the pillars
of bone that arch and spool like a cocoon.

If I lie flat and stretch out my splayed feet
I can touch his ribs, play the concertina
of their breath. And then I know happiness,
held in a minor key or, as now, drumming thumbs
against the taut and ivory skin of their brow.

His panting chest has me to handle, dead weight
in the adjacent room. I squint straight ahead
but can't decipher one red from another,
untangle threads of satin warp, aortic weft.

And this is as I would have it, though a voice
tunnels from the other side, reassuring me
the hood is intact, that I am alive,
my grandmother too. They have plans
to make me fill his belly with stones,
drag his heavier heart to a glottal stop.

But wolf and me are in this blood bath
together. He arranges knowledge in a swan-song,
music I'll not let him suffer alone.
As womb is grave, I'll not come out
though the gamekeeper and granny
call over my body, each to each.

Part 3: The Craft of Light Verse

In the first half of the 20th century, the two most highly regarded practitioners of light verse in the English language were the Americans Phyllis McGinley and Ogden Nash. In the second half of the century the most popular writer in this genre is probably the Englishman Roger McGough, whose writing is too well known to need inclusion here. The Australian poet Bruce Dawe has also written a great deal of light verse. In this section, however, three younger poets are represented – all, as it happens, from England.

Wendy Cope – 1945-

Wendy Cope is well known in Britain as a performance poet and parodist. She was a primary teacher for some years. Her best known book is *Making Cocoa for Kingsley Amis* (Faber, 1986); she has also written a verse narrative, *The River Girl* (Faber, 1991) and another collection of light verse, *Serious Concerns* (Faber, 1992).

Engineers' Corner

Why isn't there an Engineers' Corner in Westminster Abbey? In Britain we've always made more fuss of a ballad than a blueprint. ...How many schoolchildren dream of becoming great engineers?

Advertisement placed in *The Times* by the Engineering Council

We make more fuss of ballads than of blueprints –
That's why so many poets end up rich,
While engineers scrape by in cheerless garrets.
Who needs a bridge or dam? Who needs a ditch?

Whereas the person who can write a sonnet
Has got it made. It's always been the way,

For everybody knows that we need poems
And everybody reads them every day.

Yes, life is hard if you choose engineering –
You're sure to need another job as well;
You'll have to plan your projects in the evenings
Instead of going out. It must be hell.

While well-heeled poets ride around in Daimlers,
You'll burn the midnight oil to earn a crust,
With no hope of a statue in the Abbey,
With no hope, even, of a modest bust.

No wonder small boys dream of writing couplets
And spurn the bike, the lorry and the train.
There's far too much encouragement for poets –
That's why this country's going down the drain.

Triolet

I used to think all poets were Byronic -
Mad, bad and dangerous to know.
And then I met a few. Yes it's ironic –
I used to think all poets were Byronic.
They're mostly wicked as a ginless tonic
And wild as pension plans. Not long ago
I used to think all poets were Byronic –
Mad, bad and dangerous to know.

Reading Scheme

Here is Peter. Here is Jane. They like fun.
Jane has a big doll. Peter has a ball.
Look, Jane, look! Look at the dog! See him run!

Here is Mummy. She has baked a bun.
Here is the milkman. He has come to call.

Here is Peter. Here is Jane. They like fun.

Go Peter! Go Jane! Come, milkman, come!
The milkman likes Mummy. She likes them all.
Look, Jane, look! Look at the dog! See him run!

Here are the curtains. They shut out the sun.
Let us peep! On tiptoe Jane! You are small!
Here is Peter. Here is Jane. They like fun.

I hear a car, Jane. The milkman looks glum.
Here is Daddy in his car. Daddy is tall.
Look, Jane, look! Look at the dog! See him run!

Daddy looks very cross. Has he a gun?
Up milkman! Up milkman! Over the wall!
Here is Peter. Here is Jane. They like fun.
Look, Jane, look! Look at the dog! See him run!

Sophie Hannah □ 1971-

Born in Manchester, Sophie Hannah has published two volumes of light verse, *The Hero and the Girl Next Door* (Carcanet, 1995), and *Hotels Like Houses* (Carcanet 1996).

Symptoms

Although you have given me a stomach upset,
weak knees, a lurching heart, a fuzzy brain,
a high-pitched laugh, a monumental phone bill,
a feeling of unworthiness, sharp pain
when you are somewhere else, a guilty conscience,
a longing, and a dread of what's in store,
a pulse rate for the *Guinness Book of Records* –
life now is better than it was before.

Although you have given me a raging temper,
insomnia, a rising sense of panic,
a hopeless challenge, bouts of introspection,
raw, bitten nails, a voice that's strangely manic,
a selfish streak, a fear of isolation,
a silly smile, lips that are chapped and sore,
a running joke, a risk, an inspiration –
life now is better than it was before.

Although you have given me a premonition,
chattering teeth, a goal, a lot to lose,
a granted wish, mixed motives, superstitions,
hang-ups and headaches, fear of awful news,
a bubble in my throat, a dare to swallow,
a crack of light under a closing door,
the crude, fantastic prospect of forever –
life now is better than it was before.

Summary of a Western

We see a dusty desert scene and that's
The way the film begins. Some men in hats
Deliver gritty lines. They all wear braces.
They're cool and tough. They hate the darker races
Who paint peculiar stripes across their faces.

Goodies meet baddies, mostly in corrals.
Cowboys ignore or patronise their gals.
We see a gun twirl in a macho hand.
Who's killing whom we don't quite understand –
There's always some vague reference to the land.

Women in aprons have to be protected.
Stagecoaches fall. New sheriffs are elected.
The cast consists primarily of horses –
They gallop to the ending, which of course is
A happy one, where nobody divorces.

A Day Too Late

You meet a man. You're looking for a hero,
Which you pretend he is. A day too late
You realise his sex appeal is zero
And you begin to dread the second date.

You'd love to stand him up but he's too clever –
He knows by heart your work and home address.
Last night he said he'd stay with you forever.
You fear he might have meant it. What a mess!

That's when you start regretting his existence.
It's all his fault. You hate him with a passion.
You hate his love, his kindness, his persistence.
He's too intense. His clothes are out of fashion.

Shortly you reach the stage of desperation.
At first you thought about behaving well
And giving him an honest explanation.
Now all you want to say is 'Go to Hell',

And even that seems just a touch too gentle.
Deep down, the thing that makes you want to weep
Is knowing that you once felt sentimental
About this wholly unattractive creep.

Credit For The Card

She took the credit for the card I sent.
It's bad enough that you are hers, not mine.
How dare she, after all the time I spent
Choosing and writing out your Valentine,
Pretend it came from her, after the date
And its significance had slipped her mind?
She saw her chance before it was too late
And claimed my card – mysterious, unsigned –
Became the face behind my question mark.

Now there's too much at stake. She can't confess.
She has conspired to keep you in the dark
Which fact, she knows, would make you like her less.
Her lips are sealed. She lied and she forgot
Valentine's Day. I didn't. Mine are not.

Tim Hopkins – 1943-

Tim Hopkins has yet to publish a book, but his poems have appeared in several periodicals and anthologies.

Snowy Woods Revisited

Whose woods these are I think I know,
His HQ's in the City though,
Securicameras film us here,
Our trespasses in court to show.

My little son says, 'Dad, it's queer,
The owner never visits here.'
I chide, 'Don't come the William Blake,
The shares are up - we shouldn't sneer.'

He gives his doubting head a shake:
'But surely, Dad, there's some mistake
When we can't stop and take a peep
At snow-lined trees and frozen lake.'

They're selling high and buying cheap
Who from the poor this beauty keep:
The devil laughs, the angels weep,
The devil laughs, the angels weep.

The Bystander

I am part of the pollster's sample,
But never the single voice,
The also-ran at the interview,
But never the final choice.

The reflex, never the stimulus,
The shadow, but not the soul,
The splinter, the shard, or the fragment,
The fraction, but not the whole.

The actor playing a minor part,
Who's not in the press reviews,
The unknown face you see in the crowd,
When somebody else makes news.

I'm a pencilled note in the margin,
But never the text itself,
The mortice, the tenon or dovetail,
But never the actual shelf.

The padding to fill out a story,
The flesh, but not the bone,
The adjunct, addendum, appendage,
The setting, but not the stone.

One vibrant voice in the cheering crowd,
At somebody else's game,
One pair of hands in the world's applause
For somebody else's fame.

What the Papers Say: O T H E L L O

GIRL WITH EVERYTHING ASKS FOR MOOR

SOME OF MY BEST FRIENDS ARE
CHILD-ABDUCTORS SENATOR CLAIMS

DIRTY TRICKS IN ARMY PROMOTION SCANDAL

CO's BRIDE IN SEX GAMES QUERY

WIFE SMOTHERED AFTER HANKIE HANKY-PANKY

HIT-MAN FLUFFS CYPRUS CONTRACT

MAN WITH BRIEFS IN DEAD
WOMAN INNOCENT SHOCK

GENERAL DESPAIR IN
EASTERN MEDITERRANEAN

**SUICIDE SOLDIER IN MISUSE
OF ARMY WEAPONS PROBE**

Designer Pets

A cog or a dat would suit me fine,
With vices absent as virtues combine:
The feline hygiene, the canine devotion –
Someone else gets the crap and the lack of emotion.

Cat

Alluringly distant,
Seductively cool,
Disarmingly playful
But nobody's fool.

Endearingly wilful,
Aloof from the crowd,
Bewitchingly haughty,
And famously proud.

This lovable tyrant,
Beguiles and unnerves,
And makes of his master
A minion who serves.

The Moments in Between

The lemon light of daybreak is the sunset glowing red,
The seed-corn in the furrow has the scent of baking bread,
The acorn freshly planted forms a canopy of green
When we take away the moments in between.

The houses we're constructing have their demolition planned,
The ocean's rocky shoreline is a level beach of sand,
The unworked clay is Wedgwood; uncut stone, a figurine
When we take away the moments in between.

Dr Johnson dines with Plato, Buddha counsels Henry Ford,
David's slingstone fells Carnera, Custer routs the Mongol horde,
Isaac Stern duets with Nero, Dante pines for Norma Jean
When we take away the moments in between.

The hour of our birth is the hour of our death,
The first bewildered cry is the last defiant breath,
Eternity's the instant where the infinite is seen
When we take away the moments in between.

Explanatory Notes

Part I: Sixteen Poets, Fifteen Countries

Bei Dao

Declaration
Yu Luoke was a young writer accused of violating socialist policy when he argued that social class is not necessarily inherited. He was executed in 1970 about six years before the end of the Cultural Revolution.

Requiem
On June 4th, 1989, Chinese troops fired on students demonstrating for democratic reforms in Tiananmen Square, Beijing.

A Picture
Tiantian, the nickname given to the poet's daughter, is written with two characters – which look like a pair of windows. The same character also forms a part of the character for the word 'picture'.

The Bell
The three-mile storm: the students' parades along Peking's main street, Changan Avenue. This, like *Declaration*, was written in the aftermath of the Tiananmen Square massacre.

Sujata Bhatt

The Langur Coloured Night
Langur: a large, long-tailed monkey, the sacred in India.

What Happened to the Elephant
Shiva: also known as The Destroyer, one of the three main Hindu gods, the others being Brahma and Vishnu.
Ganesh: elephant-headed god who dispenses wisdom. Ganesh is the son of Shiva and his wife Parvati, and acts as guardian at the gate of his mother's house. According to the story, one day Parvati went to have her bath and told Ganesh to guard the door. He did this, even against his father, who became so angry that he decapitated Ganesh. Parvati was so upset that in order to pacify her Shiva replaced the head with the first he came across, which happened to be the head of an elephant.

Muliebrity
The title means womanhood, having the characteristics of a woman.

Oranges and Lemons
Anne Frank's House in Amsterdam is now a museum. Her diary kept during the years of the German Occupation is on display there.

Wine from Bordeaux
vierzehn Mark: 14 marks
Chernobyl: On April 26th, 1986, an atomic power station at Chernobyl in the Ukraine experienced a massive meltdown which devastated the neighbouring region and sent clouds of

radioactive dust across Europe, as far away as western France and even Wales. Vineyards in France and pastures in Wales were affected.

Orpheus Confesses to Eurydice

Orpheus was the son of the Muse of Poetry, Calliope. The god Apollo (in some versions the true father of Orpheus) presented him with a lyre and the Muses taught him to play it. Whenever he played and sang, all creation would listen entranced. As Shakespeare wrote:

> Orpheus with his lute made trees
> And the mountain tops that freeze
> Bow themselves when he did sing.
> *(King Henry VIII, III.i.3)*

When his wife Eurydice was bitten by a snake and died, Orpheus descended into the Underworld and by the power of his music persuaded Hades to let him take Eurydice back to earth. Hades imposed one condition: Orpheus must not look back at his wife until they were both on the surface of the earth. As be emerged into the sunlight, Orpheus glanced over his shoulder, and Eurydice was drawn back into the Underworld. Later, Orpheus was torn limb from limb by infuriated women in Thrace. They threw his head, which was still singing, into a river, whence it was borne into the Aegean Sea and eventually washed up on the island of Lesbos. (See also poems in this collection by Ivan Lalić and Donald Justice.)

Nina Cassian

Evolution

memento mori: reminder of death; *polenta:* a thick porridge made from maize

Ballad of the Jack of Diamonds

Donatello: 1386-1466, Italian sculptor, one of the leading figures of the Renaissance in Italy.

Charles Causley

Lord Sycamore

Pusser – Charles Causley has provided the following note for *Imagined Corners*. "*Pusser* derives from 'purser' (purser = paymaster). 100% naval (slang). It's lower deck slang, once spoken, never forgotten! The poor bloke in the poem is about to be hanged."

Ballad of the Bread Man

Gabriel: An archangel who in the Bible is God's messenger to Mary, telling her that she will bear the baby Jesus.

The Question

A hauntingly enigmatic poem, almost a succession of riddles. The poem has some of the same elliptical qualities as the folk carol from the 15th century, which seems to combine elements of the legend of the Holy Grail and the eucharist:

> Over yonder's a park, which is newly begun:
> *All bells in Paradise I heard them a-ring,*
> Which is silver on the outside and gold within:
> *And I love sweet Jesus above all thing.*
> And in that park there stands a hall:
> Which is covered all over with purple and pall:
> And in that hall there stands a bed:
> Which is hung all round with silk curtains so red:

> And in that bed there lies a knight:
> Whose wounds they do bleed by day and by night:
> At that bedside there be a stone:
> Which our blest Virgin Mary knelt upon:
> At that bed's foot there grows a thorn:
> Which was never so blossomed since Christ was born:

Carol Ann Duffy

What Price?
This poem appears to have been triggered by the so-called *Hitler Diaries*, which turned out to be a forgery.

Originally
Skelf: a splinter.

Odysseus Elytis

from **The Gloria**
The Gloria is the third and final part of Elyltis's long poem, *The Axion Esti*, a kind of spiritual autobiography. The first part, *The Genesis*, deals with the birth and growth of awareness of the narrator, or, better, the persona adopted by Elytis for this purpose; the second part, *The Passion*, deals with the persona's experiences in the Second World War and its aftermath; the third part, from which this excerpt is taken, is a long hymn of praise for the beauties still to be found in the world, despite the evils revealed in the second part.

Minium: red lead.

meltemi: a north wind that blows in the eastern Mediterranean during summer.

Myrto: Like the name Kyra (below), Myrto is the name of a girl belonging to the poet's 'personal mythology', as he has called it.

Sifnos, Amorgos etc: Aegean islands.

Zeus: The king of the gods in Greek Mythology.

Hera of the tree's ancient trunk: Hera, wife of Zeus, was the goddess of fertility and vegetation.

Kyra-Penelope: Penelope was the wife of Odysseus. During his ten years of wandering after the Trojan War, she kept suitors at bay by agreeing to choose another husband once she had finished weaving a shroud. Each night she unravelled what she had woven by day, and so avoided choosing. For the Greeks she was a symbol of wifely faithfulness. Kyra-Penelope is a deliberately ambiguous reference to both Odysseus's wife and any modern peasant woman who bears the same name.

Cyricus and Julitta: martyrs of the Greek Orthodox faith.

Hail, Girl Burning... These lines are addressed, according to the poet, "to the girl-child who will save the world and who personifies the poetic idea".

Serpent's belt of stars: a reference to the constellation known as Serpent.

Daedalic: artistic, skilful.

The Sleep of the Brave
Erebus: In Greek mythology, the son of Chaos and Darkness. Because he aided the Titans in their battle against the gods, he was cast into the infernal regions, which henceforth were sometimes known by the name of Erebus.

U A Fanthorpe

Case History: Allison (head injury)
Degas: French Impressionist, famous for his paintings of the ballet.

Not My Best Side
Reproductions of Uccello's 'St George and the Dragon' are easy to obtain. Two school texts that contain it are: *Double Vision* ed Michael and Peter Benton (London: Hodder, 1990) and *Postcards from Planet Earth* ed Paul Richardson and Ken Watson (Melbourne: Oxford University Press, 1990). Incidentally, the poet seems to have made a mistake when she has the dragon complain that the painter "left off two of my feet". The dragon in the painting is a wyvern, a two-legged, winged dragon with a serpent's tail.

Sunderland Point and Ribchester
Sunderland, Ribchester and the river Ribble are all in Lancashire, England. When *-chester* is found as part of an English place name it means that the town was once the site of a Roman camp (*castra* is the Latin for 'camp').

Halley's Comet 1985-86
Harold and his star-crossed Saxons: Halley's Comet is shown on the Bayeux Tapestry, which records the Norman invasion of England.

Giotto: Renaissance artist, famous among other things for his ability to draw a perfect circle with one sweep of the band.

Kepler: German astronomer (1571-1630) Kepler formulated the Jaws of planetary motion.

Nativities
the world cow: In Germanic mythology, the world was a barren icy waste until the primeval cow Audumla licked a block of salty ice from which the first manlike creature, a giant called Buri, emerged. Buri's son Bor was the father of Odin, the chief Norse god. Heitsi-Eibib, a deity of the African Hottentots, was the offspring of a cow. In various mythologies godlings were suckled by mares and goats, and of course Romulus and Remus, the legendary founders of Rome, were suckled by a wolf.

Blossom of oak...: Blodenwedd, of Welsh legend, was made of the blossoms of oak, broom and meadowsweet.

through the paternal/Skull fully armed: Athena sprang into being fully formed and fully armed when Hephaistos, the smith on Mount Olympus, split the skull of Zeus with an axe.

hatch from an egg: The Hindu god Brahma was said to have sprung from a golden egg.

foam-born/In Cyprus, in a shell: the birth of Aphrodite (See the famous painting by Botticelli).

Miroslav Holub

Minotaur's Thoughts on Poetry / The Minotaur's thoughts on poetry
The Minotaur, a monster with a bull's head and a man's body, dwelt in the Labyrinth in the palace of King Minos of Crete. He was slain by the Athenian hero Theseus.

... *A severed head/ may sing:* yet another reference to the story of Orpheus (see note on Sujata Bhatt).

Ivan Lalic

How Orpheus Sang
See note on Sujata Bhatt's *Orpheus Confesses to Eurydice*, p138.

Requiem for a Mother
The Holderlin epigraph translates: *Light of love! shine also on the dead, you golden one!*

Of Eurydice
See note on Sujata Bhatt's *Orpheus Confesses to Eurydice* p138.

Letter from the Knight Sinadin
When the Mongols swept into Asia Minor in 1402, the Turks and troops from the Balkans fought side be side against the invaders. They were, however, defeated in the Battle of Angora (present-day Ankara).

Princip on the Battlefield
On June 28th, 1914, Gavrilo Princip assassinated the Austrian Archduke Franz Ferdinand and his wife, thus providing the trigger for the First World War. The event occurred on the anniversary of the Battle of Kosovo in 1389, in which the Serbs were defeated by the Turks, thus causing much of the Balkans to fall under Turkish domination. Francis R Jones, in his notes on the poems in *A Rusty Needle*, tells us that on one of a cycle of poems on Kosovo Lalić tells of a girl who has been given three items by three brothers, one of whom she is to wed: a wedding ring, a coat of many colours, and a golden shawl. Searching the battlefield after the slaughter, she discovers that all three have died.

The Argonauts
In Greek mythology, a band of heroes chosen by Jason to sail in quest of the Golden Fleece. Their ship was the *Argo*.

Young Woman from Pompeii
On 24 August, 79 AD, Pompeii, a city southeast of Naples, was engulfed when Mount Vesuvius erupted. When excavations were begun in the 18th century, the bodies of many of the dead were found almost perfectly preserved by fallen ash and mud.

Gwyneth Lewis

Flyover Elegies
the circles / of Dante's hell: In the first part Dante's *Divine Comedy*, 'Inferno', the poet dreams that he is led by Virgil into Hell, which is conceived as a conical funnel, to successive circles of which the various categories of sinners are confined. Over the entrance to Hell are inscribed the words: *Abandon hope all ye who enter here*. At the lowest circle are to be found the worst criminals of history. *The Divine Comedy* was written at the beginning of the fourteenth century.

The Reference Library
Whin: whinstone – dark-coloured rocks such as dolerite or basalt.

Feverfew: a perennial plant of the chrysanthemum family, sometimes used as a herbal medicine.

logorrhoea: a mental disorder characterised by excessive talking.

Pentecost
Pentecost: Jewish harvest festival; a Christian festival celebrating the descent of the Holy Ghost upon the apostles at the time of the Jewish Pentecost.

glossolalia: either 'meaningless babble' or 'the gift of tongues'.

Torah: the teachings of the early Jewish priests; the Pentateuch, the five books of Jewish law.

Good Dog!
Om: a mantric syllable indicating the supreme principle, often chanted in order to produce a trancelike state.
Something there is about a dog/draws conversation from frosty men: Possibly a jokey reference to Robert Frost and his poem *Mending Wall*, which begins:
>Something there is that doesn't love a wall ...

Mudrooroo
A Righteous Day and *The Ultimate Demonstration*
Two poems written on the occasion of the Australian Bicentennial in 1988.

Dennis O'Driscoll
Fruit Salad
Cordate: heart shaped.

János Pilinszky
Passion of Ravensbruck
Ravensbruck was a concentration camp in Germany during the Second World War. About 50,000 women, many of whom were used in medical experiments, died there.
Revelations VIII 7
The first angel sounded, and there followed hail and fire mingled with blood, and they were cast upon the earth: and the third part of trees was burnt up, and all green grass was burnt up.
>**Bible,** King James Version (New Testament)

Tadeusz Różewicz
Mars
Mars was the Roman god of war.

Vittorio Sereni
A Dream
Sereni was born in Luino, a small town on Lake Maggiore near the Swiss border. The place names in the poem refer to this area.
Madrigal to Nefertiti
The wife of the Egyptian Pharaoh Amenhotep IV (Akhenaten) in the 14th century BC. The portrait head of Nefertiti in the Berlin museum is one of the greatest works of art to survive from ancient Egypt.
From Holland
See note on Sujata Bhatt's poem, *Oranges and Lemons* p137.

Part 2 - Variations on Traditional Themes

Donald Justice
Orpheus Opens His Morning Mail
See note on Sujata Bhatt's *Orpheus Confesses to Eurydice*, p138.

Gwen Strauss
Cinderella
The version of *Cinderella* referred to here is that by the Brothers Grimm, not by Perrault.

Part 3 - The Craft of Light Verse

Wendy Cope
Engineers' Corner
The reference here is to the Poets' Corner in Westminster Abbey, London. The Poets' Corner contains memorials to Britain's greatest writers.

Triolet
Lady Caroline Lamb described the poet Lord Byron as "mad, bad and dangerous to know". A *triolet*: Originally a French verse form, it has eight lines and two rhymes. The first line is repeated as the fourth, and the second and final lines are alike.

Reading Scheme
The form Wendy Cope has adopted for this parody of a well known early reading scheme is the villanelle, in which there are usually five three-line stanzas with an a-b-a rhyming scheme, and a final four-line stanza using the same rhymes. Note that each line has ten syllables.

Tim Hopkins
Snowy Woods Revisited
Robert Frost's well-known poem, *Stopping by Woods on a Snowy Evening*, is the starting point for Hopkins' poem.

The Moments in Between
David's slingstone fells Carnera: Primo Carnera, an Italian heavyweight boxer, was over two metres tall and weighed 127 kilos. He was heavyweight world champion in 1934, but he lost the crown in the following year to Joe Louis. He began his career as a strong man in circuses in Europe, but settled in the USA when his boxing career took off.
Isaac Stern: famous American violinist.
Norma Jean: Marilyn Monroe was christened Norma Jean.

Cross-Comparisons

The Orpheus/Eurydice Story
(See explanatory note to Sujata Bhatt's *Orpheus Confesses to Eurydice*.)
Sujata Bhatt: *Orpheus Confesses to Eurydice* p14.
Ivan Lalić: *How Orpheus Sang* p69.
                     Of Eurydice p72.
Donald Justice   *Orpheus Opens His Morning Mail* p121.

The fact that three poets in this collection have taken the Orpheus myth as their subject matter testifies to its power. The story has been reworked many times by writers (and film directors); a recent example is the Salman Rushdie novel, *The Ground Beneath Her Feet*. Why does it have such power?

Ballads Ancient and Modern
W H Auden was another 20th century poet who frequently returned to the ballad form. Ballads by Auden which can be set beside the Causley poems in this collection include *O what is that sound that so thrills the ear, Lady, weeping at the crossroads, James Honeyman*. Nina Cassian's *Ballad of the Jack of Diamonds* can be compared with Causley's ballads. Some traditional ballads that could be grouped for study with those of Causley and Auden are *Edward Edward, The Three Ravens, Lord Randal, The Twa Corbies*.

The Dramatic Monologue
Many of the poets included in *Imagined Corners* have made use of the dramatic monologue. What are the advantages of this form?

Explore the similarities and differences between the dramatic monologues of Carol Ann Duffy (*What Price?, Head of English, Yes Officer, Selling Manhattan*) and Ivan Lalić's poems (*Orpheus Confesses to Eurydice; Young Woman From Pompeii; Princip on the Battlefield; Of Eurydice; Letter from the Knight Sinadin*). You might also consider Bei Dao's *Declaration* and U A Fanthorpe's *Case History: Alison (head injury)*.

Wolf
The wolf, much maligned in folk and fairy tales, features in this collection in three poems: János Pilinszky's *Fable*, Gwen Strauss's *The Waiting Wolf* and Sue Stewart's *Inside Wolf*. The contrast between *Fable* and the cultural expectations that the topic engenders is such that the poem can very usefully be introduced by exposing the stanzas one at a time on an overhead projector and asking readers to predict how the poem will develop. Related reading: *Never Cry Wolf* by Farley Mowat and *Wolf* by Gillian Cross.

Cinderella
In addition to the poems by Sue Stewart and Gwen Strauss, there is a fine poem by the American Anne Sexton. And of course the Cinderella story is the basis of innumerable novels and films.

Anne Frank
Anne Frank's diary has had a worldwide impact, as evidenced by the fact that both Sujata Bhatt (*Oranges and Lemons*) and Vitorio Sereni (*From Holland: Amsterdam*) have written about the house where she hid for so long. The house is now a museum. The English poet Andrew Motion has also written a poem on the subject, *Anne Frank Huis*.

The Argonauts
Ivan Lalić's poem can usefully be set alongside Tennyson's famous poem, *Ulysses*, which ends with the line:

> To strive, to seek, to find, and not to yield.

Grass
Różewicz's poem pairs well with the American Carl Sandburg's poem *Grass*.

Other Suggestions for Discussion

1. The translations of Miroslav Holub's poems invite discussion of the subtle differences that result from different word choices. Detailed comparison of two versions of the one poem could be undertaken in pairs or small groups and then discussed in the whole-class situation.

2. Several of the poets in this collection, notably Pilinszky and Różewicz, have been formed by horrific experiences during the Second World War. What similarities and differences do you find between the poems of Pilinszky and Różewicz that reflect on those experiences? How does the work of these poets contrast with Causley's war poems *Recruiting Drive* and *At the British War Cemetery, Bayeux*?

3. Many, perhaps most, of the poems in this collection are susceptible to a range of interpretations. For example, even an apparently straightforward poem like Causley's *Recruiting Drive* has its puzzling elements: why is the fair 'freezing', the sea 'scribbling', the wood 'magic'? Choose two such poems and explore the range of possible meanings.

4. Examine the use of a single controlling metaphor, particularly in Charles Causley's *Lord Sycamore*, but also in János Pilinszky's *Fish in the Net*.

5. Christ's birth is directly the subject of Charles Causley's *Ballad of the Bread Man* and U A Fanthorpe's *Nativities*, but the topic is in both cases treated in an unusual way. How would you describe the tone of each? Do you consider the tone appropriate to the topic?

6. While Part 3 of *Imagined Corners* focuses directly on light verse, some of the poems in Part I could also be labelled 'light verse'. If you were choosing four poems from Part I to be included in a collection of light verse, which four would you choose? Why?

7. Many of the poems in the collection explore changes within an individual. Look closely at one of two of Nina Cassian's or Carol Ann Duffy's poems from this point of view.

8. Another theme to found in several places in *Imagined Corners* is that of alienation. Choose two poems for discussion that reflect alienation – from other individuals, from society in general, or from place.

9. Mudrooroo's *A Righteous Day* is clearly a protest poem, but would the label also fit Sujata Bhatt's *Wine from Bordeaux*? Explore the differences in tone between the two poems.

10. Odysseus Elytis has written: "The common characteristic of all poets is their dissent from current reality." Look at the work of two or three of the poets from this point of view.

11. Satire ridicules the follies of humans or their institutions. Would you agree that the term 'satire' applies to the following: U A Fanthorpe's *Reports* and *You Will be Hearing from Us Shortly*, Charles Causley's *Ballad of the Bread Man*, Dennis O'Driscoll's *Looking Forward* and *Operation*? What tools of satire do the poets make use of?

12. Some of the poems in this collection deal with displacement, physical or mental, for example, Sujata Bhatt's *The One Who goes Away*, Carol Ann Duffy's *Never Go Back* and *Originally*. Explore the attitudes and feelings expressed in each.

13. Some critics feel that the main thrust of post-World War II poetry has been to extend the range of poetry and break down conventional expectations; others see the movement as increasingly inward, concerned with exploring private anxieties Find and analyse at least one example of each tendency.

14. There are some poems in *Imagined Corners* that are about animals. Do they resemble one another in their attitude to the animals they describe? Look at Sujata Bhatt's *The Langur Coloured Night* and *The Stare*, Nina Cassian's *The Couple*, Gwyneth Lewis's *Good Dog*.

15. Is light verse necessarily superficial?

Some suggestions for writing

1. Using Wendy Cope's poems as models, try to write your own triolet and villanelle.

2. Compare the modern ballads in the book with some traditional ballads, and then write your own.

3. Ted Hughes did not speak or read Hungarian, but shaped his 'translations' of János Pilinszky's poetry by working on literal translations provided by János Csokits and other Hungarians. In order to experience at first hand the sort of task confronting Hughes, try to forge your own 'translation' of one of the poems in this book. For example, you might like to try to rewrite Nina Cassian's *Ballad of the Jack of Diamonds* in the traditional ballad metre (a four-line stanza containing alternating four-stress and three-stress lines). Charles Causley's *Lord Sycamore* is an example, though it contains some subtle variations.

4. Write the other side of the interrogation implied in Carol Ann Duffy's *Yes, Officer*.

5. Using the technique of repetition of one powerful word (*City Suburban Lines*), write your own poem on the theme of Dennis O'Driscoll's *In Office*. Or, if you prefer, write on the monotony of some other occupation.

6. Add some stanzas to Dennis O'Driscoll's *Fruit Salad*, trying to match his lush imagery.

7. With the example of Sophie Hannah's *Summary of a Western* before you, write a summary of another Hollywood genre.

8. One of U A Fanthorpe's most appealing poems, *Dear Mr Lee*, not included here, but to be found in U A Fanthorpe's *A Watching Brief*, consists of an adolescent's letter to Laurie Lee, the author of one of her set texts, *Cider with Rosie*.

> ... I just want you to know
> I used to hate English, and Mr Smart
> is roughly my least favourite person,
> and as for Shakespeare (we're doing him too)
> I think he's a national disaster..
> ....
> I wanted to say ... your book's
> the one that made up for the others...

Try your hand at a similar 'fan letter'. Try to capture a voice not your own, as U A Fanthorpe has done here.

9. Using Elytis's *Aegean* loosely as a model, write a poem in praise of a region you know.

Some Questions on Individual Poets

Bei Dao
1. Make a careful comparison of the choice of words in the two versions of *Declaration*. Which poem to you consider to be the stronger version?

2. How would you describe the tone of *Landscape over Zero*?

3. If you had to select one only of the poems of Bei Dao included in *Imagined Corners* for another multicultural anthology, which would you choose? Why?

Sujata Bhatt
1. *The One Who Goes Away* deals with a tension experienced by many who leave their homeland and settle in another country, or simply leave home. What conflicting emotions are expressed here? What is your final judgement of the poem?

2. Is *What Happened to the Elephant* simply about the 'nosy imagination' of the child?

Nina Cassian
In *Ars Poetica – A Polemic*, Nina Cassian describes her writing in these terms:
> I am subjective, intimate, private, particular
> confessional.

On the basis of the poems included here, do you agree?

Charles Causley
1. Charles Causley has said: "A poem must not be so explicit that there's no reason for the reader's imagination and sensibility to get working." Do you agree? What do you make of his poem *The Question*?

2. In the introduction to his section of *Imagined Corners*, Charles Causley is quoted as implying that his ballads have "all kinds of ironic understatements". Can you detect any of these? If so, comment on their effectiveness.

Carol Ann Duffy
1. Like several of the other poets in the collection, Carol Ann Duffy has experimented with the dramatic monologue. Which of her dramatic monologues do you find the most effective?

2. "All childhood is an emigration" (*Originally*). Explore this idea with reference to the poem.

Odysseus Elytis
"Despite his awareness of the failings of humanity and the horrors of the Second World War, Elytis is essentially optimistic, a poet who celebrates life and the beauties of the world." On the basis of the poems in *Imagined Corners*, would you agree?

U A Fanthorpe
In an interview with Eddie Wainwright (*Taking Stock*, Peterloo Poets, 1995), U A Fanthorpe said: "I try not to appear as a person myself [in my poetry]." Rather than developing "a distinctive voice", she says, she is "interested in voices .... and I enjoy working on voices for

people in the Browning way." (The Victorian poet Robert Browning wrote many dramatic monologues, the most famous of which is *My Last Duchess*.) Does the selection in *Imagined Corners* support this statement?

Miroslav Holub
Most critics of Holub note a certain surreal quality in his poetry. They also remark upon his wit. Would you agree that these are his outstanding qualities, or are there others you would highlight?

Ivan Lalic
In the dramatic monologue *Of Eurydice*, in what way do you think the speaker finds himself "hideously enriched"?

Gwyneth Lewis
1. What do you make of *Pentecost*? How would you describe its tone?
2. What do you take to be the theme of *The Reference Library*? Do you agree with Gwyneth Lewis's argument?

Mudrooroo
Which example of protest poetry do you find more effective, *The Ultimate Demonstration* or *A Righteous Day*? Why?

Dennis O'Driscoll
"The richness of O'Driscoll's imagery contrasts starkly with the bleakness of his vision." Do you find O'Driscoll's imagery rich, his vision bleak?

János Pilinszky
While Pilinszky's poetry has been greatly admired – some say that he is the greatest Hungarian poet of the post-World War II period – critics have found it difficult to explain where his greatness lies. If you like his work, try to pin down his special qualities.

Tadeusz Różewicz
Although many of his poems arise from his experiences during the Second World War, Różewicz has been described as "a permanently contemporary poet". To many readers his poems have such contemporary relevance that they seem to have been written just yesterday. Do you have this reaction? If so, try to explain it.

Vittorio Sereni
In the introduction to the Sereni selection, it is suggested that one can detect a feeling of guilt that he was not able to fight with the partisans against the fascist dictatorship. Do you agree? If so, try to pinpoint the poems and parts of poems that convey this sense of guilt. How would you describe the overall tone of his work?

Xuan Quynh
What, if anything, do the three poems of Xuan Quynh have in common?

Bibliography

Note: The starred titles are particularly recommended for inclusion in school and college libraries.

Anthologies
* **Mountain River:** *Vietnamese Poetry from the Wars*, 1948-1993 ed Kevin Bowen, Nguyen Ba Chung, Bruce Weigl. Amherst: University of Massachusetts Press, 1998
* **The Red Azalea:** *Chinese Poetry since the Cultural Revolution*, ed Edward Morin. Honolulu: University of Hawaii Press, 1990.
* **The Spaces of Hope:** *Poetry for our times and places* ed. Peter Jay. London: Anvil Press Poetry, 1998.

Individual Works
Bei Dao
* ***The August Sleepwalker.*** London: Anvil Press Poetry. 1989
* ***Old Snow.*** London: Anvil Press Poetry, 1992.
Forms of Distance. London: Anvil Press Poetry, 1994.
Landscape Over Zero. London: Anvil Press Poetry 1998

Sujata Bhatt
The Stinking Rose. Manchester: Carcanet, 1995.
* ***Point No Point:*** *Selected Poems.* Manchester: Carcanet, 1997.

Nina Cassian
* ***Life Sentence:*** *Selected Poems.* London: Anvil Press Poetry, 1990.
Take My Word for It. London: Anvil Press Poetry, 1998.

Charles Causley
* ***Collected Poems***, 1951-1975 London: Macmillan, 1975.

Wendy Cope
* ***Making Cocoa for Kingsley Amis.*** London: Faber, 1986.
The River Girl. London: Faber, 1991.
* ***Serious Concerns.*** London: Faber, 1992.

Carol Ann Duffy
* ***Standing Female Nude.*** London: Anvil Press Poetry, 1985.
* ***Selling Manhattan.*** London: Anvil Press Poetry, 1987.
The Other Country. London: Anvil Press Poetry, 1990.
* ***Mean Time.*** London: Anvil Press Poetry, 1993.

Odysseus Elytis
Selected Poems. London: Anvil Press Poetry, 1981.
* ***The Axion Esti.*** London: Anvil Press Poetry, 1980.
* ***The Sovereign Sun.*** Newcastle Upon Tyne: Bloodaxe Books, 1990.

U A Fanthorpe
Side Effects. Calstock, Cornwall: Peterloo Poets, 1978.
Standing To. Calstock: Peterloo Poets, 1982.
* ***Selected Poems.*** Harmondsworth: Penguin, 1986.

* *A Watching Brief.* Calstock: Peterloo Poets, 1987.
Neck-Verse. Calstock: Peterloo Poets, 1992.

Sophie Hannah
* *The Hero and the Girl Next Door.* Manchester: Carcanet, 1995.
* *Hotels Like Houses.* Manchester: Carcanet, 1996.

Miroslav Holub
Selected Poems. Harmondsworth: Penguin, 1967.
Notes of a Clay Pigeon. London: Secker and Warburg, 1977.
* *Poems Before and After: Collected English Translations.* Newcastle Upon Tyne: Bloodaxe Books, 1990.

Donald Justice
Orpheus Hesitated Beside the Black River. London: Anvil Press Poetry, 1998.

Ivan Lalić
Last Quarter. London: Anvil Press Poetry, 1987.
* *A Rusty Needle.* London: Anvil Press Poetry, 1996.

Gwyneth Lewis
* *Parables and Faxes.* Newcastle upon Tyne: Bloodaxe Books, 1995.
* *Zero Gravity.* Newcastle upon Tyne: Bloodaxe Books, 1998.

Mudrooroo
* *The Garden of Gethsemane.* Melbourne: Hyland House, 1991.
* *Pacific Highway Boo-Blooz.* St Lucia: University of Queensland Press, 1996.

Dennis O'Driscoll
* *Hidden Extras.* London: Anvil Press Poetry, 1987.
* *Long Story Short.* London: Anvil Press Poetry, 1993.
Quality Time. London: Anvil Press Poetry, 1997.

János Pilinszky
* *The Desert of Love.* London: Anvil Press Poetry, 1989.

Tadeusz Różewicz
* *They Came to See a Poet: Selected Poems.* London: Anvil Press Poetry, 1991.

Vittorio Sereni
* *Selected Poems.* London: Anvil Press Poetry, 1991.

Sue Stewart
* *Inventing the Fishes.* London: Anvil Press Poetry, 1993.

Gwen Strauss
* *Trail of Stones.* London: Julia MacRae Books, 1990.

Acknowledgements

Bei Dao: Anvil Press Poetry for *Declaration*, trans. Bonnie McDougall, from *The August Sleepwalker* trans. Bonnie S McDougall (1989); for *Requiem*, *A Picture*, *Gains*, *The Bell* from *Old Snow*, trans. Bonnie S McDougall & Chen Maiping (1992); and *Landscape Over Zero* from **Landscape Over Zero** (1998); David Higham Associates for *Declaration*, trans Fang Dai et al.

Sujata Bhatt: Carcanet Press for *The One Who Goes Away*, *The Langur Coloured Night*, *What Happened to the Elephant?*, *Muliebrity*, *The Stare*, *Oranges and Lemons*, *Wine from Bordeaux*, *Orpheus Confesses to Eurydice* from **Point No Point** (1997).

Nina Cassian: Anvil Press Poetry for *Evolution*, *Greed*, *Longing*, *Pain*, *I Wanted to Stay in September*, *Escape*, *The Young Bat*, *The Couple*, *Ballad of the Jack of Diamonds* from **Life Sentence**, ed. William Jay Smith (1990), and *Ars Poetica* and *Snowbound* from **Take My Word for It** (1998).

Charles Causley: David Higham Associates for *Lord Sycamore*, *Recruiting Drive*, *Ballad of the Bread Man*, *Ballad of the Faithless Wife*, *The Question*, *I Am the Great Sun*, *At the British War Cemetery, Bayeux* from **Collected Poems** (Macmillan, 1975).

Wendy Cope: Faber and Faber for *Engineers' Corner*, *Triolet*, *Reading Scheme* from **Making Cocoa for Kingsley Amis** (1986).

Carol Ann Duffy: Anvil Press Poetry for *Selling Manhattan* and *Yes Officer* from **Selling Manhattan** (1987); *Originally* from **The Other Country** (1990); *Head of English*, *What Price* from **Standing Female Nude** (1985); *Never Go Back*, *Close* from **Mean Time** (1993).

Odysseus Elytis: Anvil Press Poetry for *Aegean*, *The Sleep of the Brave*, *The Mad, Mad Boat*, *With What Stones*, *All Day Long We Walked In The Fields* from **Selected Poems** ed. Edmund Keeley and Philip Sherrard (Anvil Press Poetry, 1981) and for the excerpt from *The Gloria* in **The Axion Esti** trans. Edmund Keeley and George Savidis (1980).

U A Fanthorpe: Peterloo Poets for *Case History: Alison* and *Not My Best Side* from **Side Effects** (1978); *BC:AD*, *Reports*, *You Will Be Hearing From Us Shortly* from **Standing To** (1982); *Sunderland Point and Ribchester*, *Halley's Comet 1985-86*, *Nativities* from **A Watching Brief** (1987).

Sophie Hannah: Carcanet Press for *Credit for the Card* from **Hotels Like Houses** (1996), and for *Symptoms*, *Summary of a Western* and *A Day Too Late* from **The Hero and the Girl Next Door** (1995).

Miroslav Holub: Ewald Osers for his translations of *The Minotaur's Thoughts on Poetry* and *The Soul*; Bloodaxe Books for *Brief Reflection on Accuracy*, *Brief Reflection on Laughter*, *Brief Reflection on Test-tubes* and *Swans in Flight*, translated by Ewald Osers, from **Poems Before and After: Collected English Translations** (1990). Random House for permission to reprint the translations by J and I Milner of the following poems from Miroslav Holub's **Notes of a Clay Pigeon** (Secker and Warburg, 1977): *Brief Thoughts on Exactness*, *Brief Thoughts on Laughter*, *Brief Thoughts on a Test-tube* and *Minotaur's Thoughts on Poetry*.

Tim Hopkins: the author for *Snowy Woods Revisited*, *The Bystander*, *What the Papers Say: Othello*, *Cut*, *Designer Pets*, *The Moments in Between*.

Donald Justice: Anvil Press Poetry for *Orpheus Opens His Morning Mail* from **Orpheus Hesitated Beside the Black River** (1998).

Ivan Lalić: Anvil Press Poetry for *How Orpheus Sang*, *Ophelia*, *Requiem for a Mother*, *Of Eurydice*, *Letter from the Knight Sinadin*, *Princip on the Battlefield*, *The Argonauts*, *Young Woman* from *Pompeii* from **A Rusty Needle** trans. Francis R. Jones (1996) and for *The Spaces of Hope* from **The Passionate Measure** trans. Francis R Jones (1989).

Gwyneth Lewis: Bloodaxe Books for permission to use *Pentecost, The Reference Library* and *Fax X* from **Parables and Fares** (1995) and for *Peripheral Vision, Good Dog* and *Flyover Elegies I, II* from **Zero Gravity** (1998).

Mudrooroo: Hyland House, Melbourne, for *A Righteous Day, The Ultimate Demonstration, Tracks, Who?, Quietness, Hide and Seek* from **The Garden of Gethsemane** (1991).

Dennis O'Driscoll: Anvil Press Poetry for *Fruit Salad, In Office, Looking Forward, Operation, Case Studies* from **Long Story Short** (1993) and for *Premonitions, What She Does Not Know Is* and *Elegies* from **Hidden Extras** (1987).

János Pilinszky: Anvil Press Poetry for *Fable, Fish in the Net, The French Prisoner, Passion of Ravensbruck, The Desert of Love, Revelations VIII.7, Gradually* from **The Desert of Love**, trans. János Csokits and Ted Hughes (1989).

Tadeusz Różewicz: Anvil Press Poetry for *Mars, Abattoirs, The Survivor, Posthumous Rehabilitation, A Tree, Massacre of the Boys, Pigtail, Grass, Re-education, What Luck, Completion* from **They Came to See a Poet** trans. Adam Czerniawski (1991).

Vittorio Sereni: Anvil Press Poetry for *First Fear, Second Fear, A Dream, Six in the Morning, Those Children Playing, Madrigal for Nefertiti, Those Thoughts of Yours of Calamity, From Holland: Amsterdam* from **Selected Poems of Vittorio Sereni** trans. Marcus Perryman and Peter Robinson (1991).

Sue Stewart: Anvil Press Poetry for *Cinders* and *Inside Wolf* from **Inventing the Fishes** (1993).

Gwen Strauss: We are making every endeavour to locate the copyright holder, but to date have been unsuccessful.

Xuan Xuynh: University of Massachusetts Press for *Worried Over Days Past, The Co May Flower, Wave* from Kevin Bowan (ed), **Mountain River: Vietnamese Poetry from the Wars, 1948-1993** (Amherst: University of Massachusetts Press, 1998, Copyright © 1998 by the William Joiner Foundation).